D1597316

UNDER THE
RED STAR

UNDER THE
RED STAR

CARL-FREDRIK GEUST

Airlife

Dedication

To my friends Gena, Volodya and Zhenya, who introduced me to the fascinating history of Russian aviation.

Copyright © 1993 by Carl-Fredrik Geust

First published in the UK in 1993
by Airlife Publishing Ltd

British Library Cataloguing in Publication Data
A catalogue record for this book is available from the British Library

ISBN 1 85310 395 0

Printed by Livesey Ltd, Shrewsbury.

Airlife Publishing Ltd

101 Longden Road, Shrewsbury SY3 9EB

CONTENTS

Former LII test-pilot Mark Gallaj told the author in 1983 how disappointed he was that no rocket fuel was available for the Me 163 rocket fighter, and that thus only unpowered flights were possible.

LUFTWAFFE AIRCRAFT IN THE SOVIET AIR FORCE

One of the few remaining "black spots" in the history of aviation in the Second World War has been the testing and use of captured Luftwaffe aircraft by the Soviet Air Force.

During the war a number of German reports indicated that captured aircraft were turned against their former masters. These reports seem soon to have been forgotten, as no hard evidence was ever to be published by the Soviet side.

It has however been generally known among the specialists on Soviet aviation history that a number of German aircraft were purchased by the USSR after the signing of the infamous Ribbentrop-Molotov pact on 23 August 1939. It was naturally assumed that the Soviets tested these aircraft, but the fate of these aircraft remained unknown. Before the glasnost-years only spurious details of the delivery and testing were published in the Soviet Union. Even based on these scarce and vague facts one could but make the conclusion that the significance and impact of these deliveries on the Soviet aircraft design and production certainly must have been much greater than anticipated.

In the Soviet Union the aircraft designer and historian Vadim B. Shavrov (1898-1976), the designer Aleksandr S. Yakovlev (1906-1989), and the test-pilot Mark L. Gallaj (1914-) among others, were the first to throw light on these circumstances in their published works. There still remains some uncertainty concerning the quantity and types of aircraft delivered from Germany in 1940-41, as the published information differs in details.

Vadim Shavrov had presumably prepared a section on the testing of the German aircraft to be included in his monumental *Istoriya konstruktsii samoletov v SSSR* (History of Aircraft Construction in the USSR): Vol. 1 covering the period up to 1938 was published in three editions in 1969, 1978 and 1986, while Vol. 2 covering the years from 1938 up to 1950 has been published in two editions in 1978 and 1988. The alleged section on German aircraft of his manuscript — if existing — has however never seen the light of day.

A trickle of photographs of captured German aircraft in Soviet markings have also appeared over the years, but a comprehensive picture of the testing and use of German aircraft in the USSR has not been published in Russia — or elsewhere. The best known single account seems to be the vivid description of the testing of the war-booty Messerschmitt Me 163 as recounted by Mark Gallaj in his memoirs *Ispytany v nebe* (Tested in the Skies), first published in Russian in 1970 (a German translation *Über unsichtbare Barrieren* was published in East Germany in several editions from 1978 onwards, the fourth edition appearing in 1989).

To compile the present feature — which is the fullest treatment of the theme known — hundreds of Soviet books and articles, memoirs and biographies of Air Force commanders, pilots, engineers and designers have been perused. Wherever possible the details have also been cross-checked against German accounts and documents. The result indicates clearly that an astonishingly rich first-hand account of build and performance of German aircraft was accumulated in the USSR before, during and after the Second World War. Examples of virtually all major German aircraft types were captured and extensively test-flown during the war — the reason is easy to guess: the Soviet Air Force was naturally most interested in the performance and potential of its enemy. Undoubtedly the biggest surprise is however that these aircraft were in very many cases also used operationally!

EARLY WAR BOOTY

During the Spanish Civil War, 1936–39, several German (and Italian) aircraft were captured and test-flown by the Soviets. These included at least one Messerschmitt Bf 109B, one Heinkel He 111B, one Heinkel He 51, a number of Fiat CR 32s, and possibly even one Junkers Ju 52. At least the Bf 109B, the He 111B, the He 51 and one Fiat CR 32 were subsequently transported to the USSR for testing.

The history of these aircraft, based on the published accounts, can be summarized as follows:

A Bf 109B (Nationalist identification code 6 • 15) flown by *Feldwebel* Otto Polenz, was forced down behind the Republican lines while escorting He 111s bombing the Bujaraloz airport on 4 December 1937. This Bf 109 was tested in Spain by a French technical commission (flown among others by Capt. Constantine Rozanoff of CEMA, Villacoublay). However, because of bureaucratic blunders in the French Air Ministry, the French designers for whom the test reports were intended never did get the opportunity to see them. The aircraft was subsequently dispatched to the Soviet Union in February 1938, where it was scrupulously studied in every detail during May-June 1938 at *Nauchno-ispytatel'skij institut Voyenno-vozdushnykh Sil* or NII VVS (Research Institute of the Air Force) at Chalovskaya, from where the information certainly was passed on to those concerned. (See the Bf 109 section for details.)

The He 111 (coded 25 • 32) belonged to a formation which had taken off from Burgos de Osuma on 17 December 1937. Due to the difficult weather conditions the bomber group was scattered and the aircraft landed intact behind the Republican lines. The He 111 was likewise first tested by the French commission in February 1938 before its shipment to the Soviet Union.

Footnotes for Kopets and Zakharov (page 11)

[1] 1908-1941; Commander of the Soviet fighter group in Spain from October 1936 to June 1937, was made a Hero of the Soviet Union on 21 June 1937. During the Soviet-Finnish Winter War 1939-40 he commanded the Air Force of the 8th Army, and was finally Commander of the Air Force of the Western Military District, where he committed suicide on 23 June 1941, one day after the disastrous German surprise attack when it became clear that the AF units of the Western Military District had lost 528 aircraft on the ground and 210 in the air, out of a total of 1,200 Soviet aircraft lost during 22 June, the first day of the German attack.

[2] 1908- ; participated both in the Spanish Civil War 1936–37 and in the clashes against the Japanese in China 1938. Later Commander of 303 Istrebitel'naya aviatsionnaya diviziya, which incorporated the French voluntary Normandie-Niemen fighter regiment, Hero of the Soviet Union 19 April 1945 after scoring a total of 10 victories. Subsequently piloted a number of different captured aircraft.

A Fiat CR 32 captured by the Republican forces in Spain and later shipped to the Soviet Union for investigation in the NII VVS.

The Fiat CR 32 with Soviet insignia at the NII VVS.

According to the memoirs of Georgiy N. Zakharov, four Fiat CR 32s made forced-landings at Albacete, which was held by the Republicans. They were ferried by Ivan I. Kopets[1] and Georgiy N. Zakharov[2] to Alcala (see footnotes page 9).

This incident is however rather difficult to pin-point from available sources. One intact CR 32, code 3 • 6, piloted by Lt. Giorgio Francesci had already been captured when it force landed at Don Benito on 16 September 1936. This aircraft was wrecked at Alcalâ de Henares in November 1936, but is obviously not referred to by Zakharov, who does not indicate any date.

Kopets and Zakharov even made clandestine reconnaissance flights with the Fiat fighters in Spain.

The Fiat CR 32 was also flown by "General Douglas", alias Yakov V. Smushkevich.[3] One Fiat CR 32 was dispatched to the USSR for thorough testing at NII VVS in 1937. At least six Fiat CR 32s were captured intact by the Republicans during the war.

However, there does not seem to be any positive information regarding the identity of the He 51B-1 (This aircraft was captured in damaged condition, but was subsequently repaired by the Soviets and flown in simulated dogfights against the I-15 at the NII VVS). The same applies to the Ju 52 captured by the Republicans and subsequently tested by the Soviets.

Two Nakajima I-96 fighters were captured intact in China in 1938 and flown by Georgiy M. Zakharov and Aleksej S. Blagoveshchenskij.[4] The two Soviet pilots were ordered to ferry the Japanese fighters to Moscow for further examination, but the trip was aborted because of sabotage (sugar in the fuel tanks!), forcing the pilots to land at Langzhou. At least one of the aircraft was transported onwards by truck. The I-96 fighter was certainly flight tested in NII VVS together with an example of the latter variant I-97 by eg. Mikhail I. Tarakanovskiy.

In the recent history of NII VVS the dramatic testing of the Nakajima I-95 is also reported: the captured aircraft was delivered by train from Mongolia to the NII VVS at Chalovskaya, where it was first flown by Aleksey I. Kubyshkin. After the initial tests it was decided to organize a simulated dogfight between the Polikarpov I-153 Chaika and the Japanese fighter in August 1939. The People's Commissar of Defense Kliment Ye. Voroshilov and the top command of the Soviet Air Force were invited to attend the dog fight demonstration, with Kubyshkin piloting the Soviet fighter and Mikhail N. Vakhrushev (the second NII VVS test pilot to fly the I-95 after Kubyshkin) piloting the Japanese fighter.

---

[3] 1902-1941; commanded the Soviet Air Force detachment in Spain from October 1936 to June 1937, was made a Hero of the Soviet Union on 21 June 1937. In September 1939 Commander-in-Chief of the Soviet Air Force, arrested on 7 June 1941 "for treacherous activity", and executed on 28 October, 1941.

[4] 1909- ; who commanded a Soviet "voluntary" fighter group in China from December 1937 to August 1938. On return to USSR he was made a Hero of the Soviet Union 14 November 1938, after scoring a total of 7 victories in 14 combats in China. He was later to become CO of 2 *Istrebitel'nyj aviatsionnyj korpus* — 2 Fighter Aviation Corps — and serving after the war as Director of NII VVS from 1952 to 1959 in which capacity he visited Farnborough in September 1956 where he flew the two-seat Hawker Hunter T.7 with Bill Betford as co-pilot.

After chasing each other for six minutes the eagerly awaited result was finally achieved, as Kubyshkin was able to hang at the I-95's tail and take a good aim. Vakhrushev however did not want to give in, but wanted to show his best and did his utmost to escape. His violent turn resulted in a tragedy — the Japanese fighter started spinning, and at the low altitude crashed and exploded in the forest surrounding the aerodrome. After having expressed his regrets to the head of NII VVS Gen. Filin, Voroshilov departed, leaving the upset Kubyshkin mourning his test pilot colleague and friend.[5]

During the Soviet-Finnish Winter War 1939-1940 only one Finnish aircraft is known to have been captured in anything near intact condition. This aircraft was the Fokker D.21 coded FR-76, flown by Sgt. Mauno Fräntilä of LeLv 24, who made a forced landing near the front line at Vilaniemi near Viipuri (now Vyborg), after being damaged in combat with Soviet fighters on 5 March 1940. He was shot down by Capt. Nikolaj M. Kidalinskiy of 7 *Istrebitel'nyj aviatsionnyj polk* (of 59 *Istrebitel'naya aviatsionnaya brigada* which belonged to the Air Force of the 7th Army). The Finnish ground forces tried without success to destroy the aircraft after the pilot had escaped from the "no man's land", but it was removed by Soviet troops and subsequently transported to Leningrad for examination. The Fokker fighter was displayed at a war booty exhibition in Leningrad up to the beginning of the "Great Fatherland War". The further fate of FR-76 is unknown.[6]

[5] The Soviet designations "I-95", "I-96" and "I-97" correspond obviously to the following Japanese types: "I-95": Nakajima Type 95 (A4N1); "I-96": Mitsubishi Type 96 (A5M); "I-97": Nakajima Type 97 (W27).

[6] The Finnish Air Force lost 68 aircraft in the Winter War (of which 36 were in air combat, and another 8 shot down by enemy anti-aircraft artillery), while the Russians in 1989 still claimed a ridiculous number of 362 victories! When the Russians attacked on 30 November 1939 the Finnish AF had only 116 combat aircraft (of which only 36 Fokker D.21 fighters and 14 Bristol Blenheim bombers could be considered relatively modern, the other aircraft being obsolete Fokker C.Xs, Fokker C.VEs, Bristol Bulldogs, Blackburn Ripons and Junkers K43s). Although a number of aircraft were delivered during the Winter War from eg. England, France, Italy and Sweden, the number of FAF aircraft never did rise even near to the Soviet victory claim.

On the other hand, the Finnish AF claimed 190 and the Finnish anti-aircraft artillery claimed over 300 destroyed Soviet aircraft. These claims have recently been virtually verified, as a still incomplete calculation published in the *Voyenno-istoricheskiy zhurnal* (March 1992) admits losses of 579 aircraft. As the losses of a number of aviation regiments are still missing, the total losses of the Soviet AF in the Winter War is estimated to be 640–650 aircraft.

Heinkel He 51 captured by the Republican forces in Spain and later shipped to the Soviet Union for testing by the NII VVS, in the picture already with red stars.

The Finnish Fokker D.21 FR-76 (pilot Sgt. M. Fräntilä, 3/LLv 24) made a forced landing on 5 March 1940 at Säkkijärvi on the Karelian Isthmus during the Finnish-Soviet Winter War. The damaged aircraft was evacuated by Soviet troops for investigation, and was later on display at a war booty exhibition in Leningrad.

Only a few Finnish aircraft are known to have been forced down behind the Soviet lines in anything like repairable condition during the "Continuation war" 1941-44: Ensign T. Piiparinen of 2./LeLv 26 was shot down by anti-aircraft artillery over the Karelian Isthmus on 11 June 1942 and made a rather successful forced landing (note the extended under-carriage!) in his Fiat G.50 FA-14 near Lake Lempaala. He was taken prisoner by the Soviet forces and apparently died in a POW camp.

...act identity of this Brewster is unfortunately not known as the Soviet soldier is very efficiently covering the numerical identification ...t could most probably be BW-374 of Ltn T. Mattila of HLeLv 26, who did not return from his mission to Kivennapa on the ...n Isthmus on 12 June 1944.

An ex-Czechoslovak Avia B-534 biplane fighter at N▌ VVS. Note that all identification insignia have been covered.

A Focke-Wulf Fw 200 Condor (N-400) of *Polyarnaya Aviatsiya* (the identification code and the inscription are visible on the original print).

TRADE WITH GERMANY

After the Nazi-Soviet non-aggression pact signed in Moscow on 23 August 1939 (and the preceding commercial agreement already signed on 19 August 1939, granting the USSR a credit of 200 Million Reichsmark at 5 per cent interest for imports from Germany during the next two years, with reciprocal Soviet deliveries of raw-materials to the value of 180 Million RM) things developed very fast, in a real "honeymoon manner": A Soviet-German "friendship and border" pact was signed on 28 September 1939, and in the attached exchange of notes principles of commercial co-operation in military hardware were outlined, after which a Soviet military-technical purchase delegation toured the German industry, including a number of aviation factories in October-November 1939.

The delegation was headed by the exceptionally skilled engineer and industrialist Ivan F. Tevosyan (1902-1958), member of the Central Committee of the Bolshevik Party (TsK VKP(b)), and simultaneously People's Commissar for Shipbuilding Industry[7] and General of Artillery G.K. Savtshenko (who headed the Artillery Administration of the Red Army), as one of the main points of interest was modern warships and heavy (naval) artillery. It is a significant fact that Tevosyan had already visited Germany twice as a young engineer, spending some time at the Krupp steel works in Essen in the early 1930s where he learnt German.

The delegation which arrived in Berlin on 26 October 1939 had a total of 48 members, with several specialized subgroups. The aviation subgroup led by General Aleksandr I. Gusev was especially impressive; with Col. Ivan F. Petrov (Deputy Director of the *Tsentralnyy aerogidrodinamicheskiy institut* or TsAGI, the No.1 Soviet aerodynamical research institute; Petrov was to become a Major-General on 7 May 1940, and Director of the Air Force Research Institute NII VVS on 10 June 1940) as Gusev's deputy, and a number of designers whose products would cause not only the Germans much trouble in the years to come: Nikolay N. Polikarpov (1892-1944) and Aleksandr S. Yakovlev (1906-1989), and of lesser fame Vladimir V. Shevchenko (fighter designer, head of the short-lived aircraft Experimental Design Bureau OKB-30 in 1939-41).

---

[7] He was the former General Director of the Spetsstal group of steel factories, and First Deputy People's Commissar for Defence Industry, and was to be appointed People's Commissar for Ferrous Metallurgy on 2 June 1940 — an extremely important post which he was to hold for the rest of the war. After the war he was Minister of Metallurgical Industry to 1953, Deputy Prime Minister to 1956, and finally Soviet Ambassador to Japan.

The designers were assisted by production experts: Vasili P. Balandin (Director of Aircraft Engine Factory No. 26 in Rybinsk, soon to become a Deputy People's Commissar for Aircraft Industry, responsible for aircraft engine production) and Vasili P. Kuznetsov (Head of the engine department of NII VVS; also to become a Deputy People's Commissar, responsible for bomber production), the Director of the Moscow Aircraft Factory No.1 *im. Aviakhima* Petr V. Dementyev.[8]

A very capable test-pilot from NII VVS, Stepan P. Suprun[9] was also included in the delegation, together with V.K. Mikhin of the Trade Representation in Germany as commercial expert and Ms. N.N. Perglova as interpreter. The Soviet delegation met with a number of their German counterparts, including *Generalfeldmarschall* Hermann Göring, *Generaloberst* Ernst Udet, the aircraft designers Ernst Heinkel, Willy Messerschmitt and Kurt Tank, and was also able to visit the Heinkel, Messerschmitt, Dornier, Junkers and Focke-Wulf factories.

Another industrial delegation of about 16 members led by the People's Commissar for Iron and Steel Industry P.I. Korobov followed a few days later. Some of the technical experts were to spend some time in Germany, eg. the designer Aleksandr Kobzarov of the Tupolev OKB (he obviously worked in the part of the OKB not imprisoned, which was headed by Tupolev's deputy A.A.Arkhangelskiy) was sent for an over six-weeks study tour to Germany. He was later to be appointed Chief Engineer of Aircraft Factory No. 22 in Fili, which was producing SB-2 bombers.

Ernst Heinkel, who had already sold HD 55 flying-boats to the Soviets (Soviet designation KR-1) in 1930, has described the visit of the Soviet delegation to his factory in Marienehe on 30 October 1939 in his memoirs *Stürmisches Leben*. When Dipl.-Ing. Rolf Wilhelm Lucht *(Chefingeniur des Technischen Amtes* of Ernst Udet's *General-Luftzeugmeister-Amt)* surprisingly gave Heinkel instructions to receive the Soviet delegation, there were some organizational problems as a Japanese delegation, also interested in the Heinkel He 100 fighter, was to visit the Marienehe factory on the very same day, and the delegations were not to notice each other! This problem was solved by exact timing of the factory tours in addition to a minutiose reporting system — even using couriers on motorcycles. Heinkel relates how his engineers observed that the young Yakovlev tried to unnoticeably measure the aircraft dimensions by just randomly touching some parts with his hand, but in fact carefully counting hand- and fingerwidths.

After the successful visit, Heinkel was later invited to a vodka-loaded party at

---

[8] 1907-77; in 1941 he was appointed first Deputy People's Commissar for Aircraft Production. From 1953 to 1957 and from 1965 he was Minister of Aircraft Production; in the intermediate period 1957 to 1965 the ministerial organization was replaced by a State Committee for Aircraft Technology, also headed by Dementyev who retained his ministerial rank.

[9] He was made an HSU on 20 May 1940, and for the second time posthumously on 22 July 1941 after being killed in action while escorting bombers in a MiG-3 in the Borisov area on 4 July 1941 as CO of 401 IAP which consisted of test-pilots who had volunteered for combat service. He scored a total of 2 victories.

the Soviet Embassy in Berlin, where Göring was also present. Heinkel speaks only modestly of a "five-o'clock tea", but this was probably the reception given to commemorate the 22nd anniversary of the October Revolution on 7 November 1939, which was then celebrated in the exceptional "honeymoon" spirit.

When touring various factories General Gusev was suspicious and not convinced that the Germans had shown modern aircraft. The aviation experts were of different opinion and reported that they had been shown the main types of the Luftwaffe, and recommended to buy samples of certain aircraft.

In this connection Udet is cited by the Soviet aviation historian M.S. Arlazorov: "I am an officer and I am responsible for my words. We have shown you everything, and if you are not satisfied — do not buy. We do not urge you. It is your business. . ."

In his reminiscences Petrov makes very far-reaching conclusions, stating that Udet would have authorized the delivery of the modern aircraft to the Soviet Union without Hitler's knowledge. When the German dictator became aware of Udet's "treason" he would either have had Udet executed or demanded he perform suicide on 17 November 1941. This is certainly not true — when reading the published documents of the German *Auswärtiges Amt* (Foreign Office) it is evident that both the principles and the main items of the export to the USSR were authorized by Hitler himself. (That Hitler may have needed a scapegoat when the conseqences of the early deliveries of examples of the principal aircraft Luftwaffe to the future enemy became clear, as the Russian campaign stalled in autumn 1941, is another matter.)

The delegation returned to Moscow on 14 December 1939, having spent seven weeks in Germany. Upon his return from Germany Polikarpov met with an unpleasant surprise: the major part of his Design Bureau had — without his knowledge, but of course with the consent of the People's Commissariat — been separated into an independent organization! (The formal decision had been signed on 8 December 1939.) This new Design Bureau was headed by the young engineers Artyom I. Mikoyan (1905-70) and Mikhail I. Gurevich (1893-1976), and was destined to gain world fame for its MiG-named aircraft.

A second industrial delegation (with Yakovlev now leading the subgroup on aviation and Petrov once more seconding the subgroup leader) visited Germany in March 1940. The elderly Polikarpov did not get another chance to study the German technology — as his place in the delegation was now given to Mikoyan.

Yakovlev himself was to visit Germany for a third time in November 1940 as a member of the delegation of Vyacheslav M. Molotov (at that time simultaneously heading the Soviet Government and the Foreign Ministry) who met with *Reichskanzler* Adolf Hitler in Berlin on 12-13 November 1940 with the well-known disastrous results. Yakovlev remained in Germany for another 14 days touring various aircraft factories. The military-industrial specialists in Molotov's delegation were once more headed by Tevosyan (already appointed People's Commissar for Ferrous Metallurgy), and included the Deputy Head of the Operations Department of the General Staff, General A.V. Vasilevskiy (1895-1977; a future Marshal of the Soviet Union and Chief of General Staff) and General V.M. Zlobin of the People's Commissariat for Defence, among others.

At this period the young Yakovlev was a favourite of Stalin, and that the feelings were mutual can be deduced, even from the most recent editions of Yakovlev's memoirs, where his admiration of *A Great and Simple Man* (which was the title of a children's book about 'Stalin and aviation', written by Yakovlev in 1945) is only superficially concealed. Yakovlev had been handpicked by Stalin to be Deputy People's Commissar for Aviation Industry at the age of only 35 years. The dictator got to know him during the big Aviation Days at Moscow Central Airport during the "Great Terror" years 1936-38. Yakovlev's light sport aircraft had performed well, and thus on 11 January 1940 he was put in charge of "experimental aircraft construction and R&D", ie being superior of all established aircraft designers, many years his senior. That a great number of them, including the No.1. Soviet aircraft designer Andrej N. Tupolev (1888-1972) was sitting in the "engineer's prison" OKB-29 *sharaga* in Moscow under control by the infamous NKVD (People's Commissariat for Internal Affairs) because of false and ridiculous accusations — Tupolev had been arrested on 21 October 1937, and accused, among other things of having sold his designs to Germany (!) while visiting the USA in 1935 to study the American aircraft industry — does not seem to have bothered the newly-appointed Deputy People's Commissar very much.

Yakovlev was from now on continually consulted by Stalin in aviation matters, and in his memoirs he has given a vivid picture of the preparations of his repeated trips to Germany. He was even able to bother Stalin with such minute details as the per diem of the Soviet specialists (it was increased from 15 to 25 roubles per day!), but also suggesting "some changes in the composition of the delegation" (it is unclear what is hidden behind this carefully worded sentence in Yakovlev's memoirs; could this indicate that Yakovlev had Polikarpov dropped from the delegation, with Mikoyan replacing him?)

An extremely important question was that when leaving for the second trip, the shrewd Yakovlev got a letter-of-credit in his pocket allowing him to spend one million roubles for on-the-spot purchases for auxiliary equipment of his choice, with a promise of another million if needed. In case of any difficulties Yakovlev was entitled to cable Stalin directly from Germany using the code address "Ivanov, Moscow". This was obviously an unprecedented case of cutting through the red-tape of Soviet foreign-trade bureaucracy, which would have required a formal request to the Soviet trade representation in Berlin, which would have had to forward this request to the People's Commissariat for Foreign Trade in Moscow. This body in its turn would then have to consult the corresponding bureaucrats at the People's Commissariat for Aircraft Industry and the Soviet Air Force. If the complete formal procedure had been stuck to, there would have been hardly any deliveries to the USSR before 22 June 1941!

Yakovlev was in fact forced to contact Stalin from Germany, much to the annoyance of the Soviet trade representatives in Berlin who wanted to perform the import operations in their well-established, and extremely slow ways, before they believed that he really was authorized to make on-spot deals without normal formal approval by Moscow.

Here Yakovlev is however obviously exaggerating his personal importance — as meanwhile the principles of the main aircraft deliveries had been agreed upon on the highest level. The Soviet delegation did not present any lists of wanted equipment on arrival in Germany in October 1939 as promised, but only after Tevosyan and Savchenko had visited Moscow for consultations after the first round of factory tours. Their "shopping list" was brought to Germany on 30 November 1939. This list was very extensive and must have been a shock for the German political and military authorities:

1. Navy equipment
— three cruisers; of which two were under construction at German shipyards (*Seydlitz* and *Lützow*), the third being *Prinz Eugen*; and the blueprints of the battleship *Bismarck*;
— one training ship, one repair ship and one tanker;
— 31,000 tonnes of steel armour plate for shipbuilding; and
— contactless torpedoes and magnetic mines of newest design.

2. Air force equipment
— the Messerschmitt 209 fighter, and other modern aircraft which presumably exist, but which have not been shown (!), and
— modern aircraft engines (same comment as above).

As compensation the Soviet government was ready to start licence-production of the aircraft and aircraft engines indicated, and would deliver one third of the intended production to the German government.

The list goes on with artillery, ammunition, fire control equipment, and finally mentions complete industry processes (incl. production of synthetic fuel). All equipment was to be delivered as soon as possible (preferably within 1940).

The German Foreign Ministry immediately arranged (on Saturday 2 December 1939 at 12.30 hours!) an internal meeting with top level German industrial and financial executives to consider Tevosyan's list. The total value of the list (without possible licence-producing rights, which had to be calculated separately) was estimated to be 1.5 billion Reichsmarks (the naval programme alone amounted to 700 million RM, of which the three cruisers only were valued at 420 million RM). A principle decision of the Führer was considered necessary for the main items. Among the aviation items requiring Hitler's decision were mentioned possible delivery of the Me 209 and *He 110* (it is not clear whether the He 100 or the Me 110 is meant by this misprint), and the Jumo 207 and Jumo 208 engines. Fulfilment of the Soviet wishes was estimated to require 80,000 t steel per month for one whole year — when the total amount of steel available for export was 185,000 tons only!

The German standpoint was that the credit agreement of 19 August 1939 allowed military deliveries for only 59 million RM; however, if fully compensated by Soviet deliveries of raw material, military equipment to the value of up to 660 million RM could be considered.

Furthermore the Germans considered that the Russians were to perform their raw material deliveries first, after which compensating German deliveries of machinery would commence — and not in the reverse order as Tevosyan's list implied! The delivery time demanded was considered completely unacceptable (and even physically impossible), considering that Germany was at war.

After a series of tough negotiations with the Soviet representatives in Berlin on one hand, and between Molotov and the German Ambassador Graf Werner von der Schulenburg in Moscow on the other (where in particular the price demanded for the aircraft selected — 300 million RM was considered ridiculous by the Soviets) the matter was transferred to Hitler and Stalin for decision.

The final solution was ironed out in three lengthy negotiations in the Kremlin (31 December 1939, 29 January and 8 February 1940) with Stalin, Molotov, Anastas I. Mikoyan,[10] Tevosyan and Ye. Babarin (Soviet Trade Representative in Germany) representing the Soviet side, and Graf von der Schulenburg (not present on 8 February 1940), Ambassador Dr. Karl Ritter (Special Envoy of the German Foreign Ministry), Minister Dr. Karl Schnurre and Gustav Hilger (Counsellor of the German Embassy in Moscow) representing the German side. The main topics of the nightly negotiations were the naval deliveries, where a compromise was finally reached. The aircraft deliveries did not seem to cause any big problems, as possible license production was agreed to be handled later, if necessary.

The official trade agreement was finally signed by Dr. Karl Ritter and Dr. Karl Schnurre, and Anastas I. Mikoyan and Ye. Babarin in Moscow on 11 February 1940. According to this agreement Germany would deliver military and industrial equipment up to a value of 420-430 million Reichsmarks to the USSR during the period from 11 February 1940 to 11 May 1941, and up to a value of 220-230 million RM during the period 11 May to 11 August 1941 in exchange for Soviet deliveries of raw materials, metals, fuel, grain etc. (According to a Soviet article published in autumn 1989 — the compromise reached followed more the Soviet than the German proposal!)

The *Liste 2* attached to the agreement stipulated that immediate negotiations were to commence concerning delivery of the cruiser *Lützow,* technical documentation and blueprints of a number of other warships (the heavy cruisers *Seydlitz, Prinz Eugen* and *Admiral Hipper* and the battleship *Bismarck*), shipyard

---

[10] 1895-1978; People's Commissar for Foreign Trade and elder brother of the aircraft designer Artem I. Mikoyan who was yet to tour the German aircraft factories! After the war he was for many years Minister of Foreign Trade and Deputy Prime Minister.

equipment, naval engines, naval artillery, mines, hydroacoustical, hydrographical equipment. (The intensive Soviet-German naval co-operation also took other forms than direct hardware trading: a U-boat base *"Basis Nord"* at the Zapadnaya Litza Bay near Murmansk was put at *Seemarine*'s disposal!)

The trade agreement of 11 February 1940 also included optical equipment, field artillery, communications equipment, chemical equipment (incl. samples of Buna S, SS, N and NN synthetic rubber), pioneer equipment, samples of ammunition and pyrotechnical equipment, armoured vehicles (including a complete medium Pz Kpfw III tank), 308 different metal cutting machines, and an impressive list of aircraft:

    10 Heinkel "He-100"
     5 Messerschmitt 109
     5 Messerschmitt 110
     2 Junkers "Ju-88"
     2 Dornier "Do-215"
     3 Buecker "Bü-131"
     3 Buecker "Bü-133"
     3 Focke-Wulf "Fw-58-V-13"
     2 Focke-Wulf "Fa 266" helicopters.

(The aircraft designations are spelled here exactly as in the List 2 of the trade agreement!)

All aircraft were to be delivered within 15 months, fully equipped with guns, bombs, gunsights and radios; in addition one Messerschmitt 209 was to be delivered within 12 months; further aircraft engines, instruments, spares, ammunition, bombs etc. will be delivered. Within the second period of the agreement (11 May to 11 August 1941) deliveries of additional equipment for all arms is foreseen, including aircraft engine test beds, cine-photo theodolite stations and other items.

According to Shavrov the final result of the Soviet aircraft shopping was almost as planned: six (not ten) Heinkel He 100 fighters, five Messerschmitt Bf 109E fighters, five Messerschmitt Bf 110C heavy fighters, one Messerschmitt Me 209 fighter (the absolute world speed record holding aircraft!), two Dornier Do 215 B bombers, three Bücker Bü 131 Jungmann sports aircraft, three Bücker Bü 133 Jungmeister sports aircraft, three Focke-Wulf Fw 58 two-engine communication aircraft, two Focke-Achgelis Fa 266 helicopters (!), and two Fieseler Fi 156 liaison aircraft, ie. a total of 36 aircraft. It is noteworthy that Yakovlev mentions in his memoirs explicitly only five Bf 109s, two Ju 88s, two Do 215s and one He 100.

Most of the aircraft listed by Shavrov are referred to in other Soviet publications, but some aircraft *not* listed by him are also mentioned by various authors as allegedly delivered to the Soviet Union from Germany:

Dornier Do 117 and 217 (?), Heinkel He 111, Junkers Ju 52 and Ju 87, Focke-Wulf Fw 189 "Uhu" and even an Fw 190 (this is certainly a mistake; most Soviet sources are explicit that the Fw 190 was *not* delivered, which it simply could not have been in 1940, because of the early stage of its development at that time). The Russians obviously did not even see any Fw 190 prototypes during their visit. Petrov states however that the Russians luckily refused to buy the offered Focke-Wulf Fw 190 and Dornier Do 217, which "were not to be very widely used at the front". He mentions nothing of the major purchase of the Russians — the Heinkel He 100, which was not used operationally at all by the Germans.

Shavrov's list is probably correct, and the other aircraft types indicated by other Soviet authors might be war-booty captured at various phases of the war. (Note: the two Dornier bombers were in fact of the Do 17Z subtype, assigned the special export designation Do 215 B-3.)

Yakovlev's second trip to Germany (March 1940) was of course directly related to the execution of the trade agreement signed on 11 February 1940. Col. Ivan Petrov states explicitly that he (Petrov) was authorized to perform the purchase and organize the dispatch of the aircraft to Moscow.

Petrov also explains the significance of Yakovlev's "pocket money", which was to be used for "on-the-spot" purchases of auxiliary equipment, not foreseen in the main trade agreement. "And who would know better than we, the Deputy People's Commissar and Deputy Director of NII VVS what we need?"

For this "pocket money" auxiliary airfield equipment, cross-country vehicles, automobiles, technical literature, equipment for the manufacture of Kuhlmann drawing tables and other items were acquired.

An interesting point is that some of the equipment obviously personally chosen by the Artillery General G.K. Savchenko (No.2 of the first Soviet delegation in October 1939) was to be literally turned against the Germans: when the situation of the defence of Moscow became critical in October 1941, four German heavy 105 mm anti-aircraft guns were "found" at a weapons trial ground belonging to one of the Air Defence research institutes. These heavy guns were quickly transferred to Moscow and incorporated in the air defense of the Soviet capital.

Most of the aircraft were already delivered in May-June 1940, which gave the Soviets ample time for testing them before the German attack on 22 June 1941. Some of the aircraft seem to have been directly allocated to NII VVS at Chalovskaya, where they were test-flown with emphasis on the fighting characteristics. The NII VVS engineer Izrail G. Rabkin has given a detailed picture of the thorough testing of the Bf 109E (running over 20 pages) in his memoirs published in 1985. Engineers from various Design Bureaux were invited to study the details of the German aircraft and follow the testing at NII VVS.

Apart from establishing the general characteristics and comparative parameters of the German aircraft, the experienced NII VVS specialists especially looked for weak points and deficiencies of their study objects. The German fighters were found to lack some vertical manoeuvrability, the bombers had no armoured protection and weak defensive armament. The small size of the bomb covers enabled only 50 kg bombs to be carried internally, the radiators lacked protection etc.

However, the Soviets also noted the great importance laid by the Germans on use of standardized details facilitating series production, and the "ergonomy" (although this was a completely unknow notion at that time) of the cockpit planning — even at the cost of other characteristics considered far more valuable by the Soviet designers.

Tupolev's future Deputy, Leonid L. Kerber has given a dramatic picture of the visit of the imprisoned Tupolev OKB to NII VVS at Chalovskaya ("*Tupolevskaya Sharaga*" — his manuscript was first published anonymously in West Germany in 1971, but was serialized in two Soviet journals in 1988-90). The designers were brought from their confinement at the former Aircraft Factory No.156 on Ulitsa Radio in Moscow to Chalovskaya guarded by the NKVD Major Kruchkov, Deputy Commanding — in the very literal sense of the word! — Officer of KB-103 — which was the Tupolev-led department of the NKVD-directed TsKB-29 "*sharaga*"; (the others being KB-100 led by V. Petlaykov, KB-102 led by V. Myashichev and KB-110 led by D. Tomashevich). The imprisoned "enemies of the people" (the designers had generally not been outside their *sharaga* since autumn 1937 or winter 1938 when most of them had been "invited" to TsKB-29 by the NKVD) were given an unexpected opportunity of meeting free colleagues — designers and aviators at Chalovskaya. They found many interesting technical details and good engineering solutions in the German aircraft. As the test-pilots were also present, the designers also got first hand impressions of the aircraft handling characteristics. Kerber even managed an unexpected moment to talk to his brother B.L. Kerber, who worked as an engineer in Yakovlev's OKB. Kerber's short moment of personal chat and family greetings was however soon interrupted by the NKVD guards who ordered their prisoners to go for lunch. The engineer-prisoners were paradoxically invited to the highest-rank of the five canteens at NII VVS — intended for Generals only. Three VVS generals, P.A. Lyusikov (Deputy Director of NII VVS), S.A. Danilin (who had participated in the 11,500 km Moscow-San Giacinto non-stop long-distance flight with the Tupolev-designed ANT-25 12-14 July 1937, for which he was made a Hero of the Soviet Union on 1 September 1937) and N.P. Shelimov were having lunch, and greeted their unexpected "guest of honour" A.N. Tupolev very warmly, and, trying not to allude to his situation, wanted to listen to his impression of the German aircraft. After a rather unforced professional discussion Tupolev could not refrain from giving Losyukov a well-disguised reference to his situation:

"— Prokhor Alekseyevich, it was a pleasure seeing the Me 110, 'my aircraft'!"

This parabole — clearly referring to the groundless and absurd accusations that Tupolev had sold his designs to the Germans — stopped the discussions at once, as it was completely clear to everyone what Tupolev had in mind. Under the watchful eyes of Kryuchkov, the Generals bade farewell to Tupolev, embracing him without words, as no one dared to make any comment whatsoever!

Some of the German aircraft were delivered to TsAGI at Zhukovskiy (which in the meantime had been taken over by I.F. Petrov, who was promoted to Major-

General on 7 May 1940). At TsAGI the aircraft were "flown" in the huge windtunnels and laboratories, with practical aerodynamics tested at the TsAGI flight department. This test flight body was soon (8 March 1941) to be reshaped into an independent *Letno-issledovatel'skiy institut* or LII (Flight Test Institute) headed by the legendary test pilot Mikhail M. Gromov.[11] That the study of the German aircraft had great impact on the Soviet aviation technology is without doubt (one needs only remember the professional composition of the Soviet delegations to Germany!).

Over 3,500 aviation specialists representing 21 aircraft factories, three design bureaux and also pilots and engineers of the Soviet Air Force took part in the very detailed investigation of the German aircraft at NII VVS. The main part of the investigation was performed between May and October 1940, resulting in plans for urgent modernization of the Soviet aircraft designs and aviation industry. This modernization was to be completed before 1942.

The German aircraft were delivered in crates to the Central Airport of Moscow where they were assembled under the surveillance of representatives of the German manufacturers!

The Soviet aviation historian M.S. Arlazorov recalls: "it was strange to see German workers with MESSERSCHMITT, JUNKERS and DORNIER in big letters on their overalls at our Central Airport in Moscow . . ." If this was strange to contemporary Russians, one cannot but make the unanswered enigmatic question why Hitler permitted the delivery of these advanced aircraft to his potential adversary in 1940. The answer probably remains forever hidden in the complex mind of the erratic dictator.

Meanwhile Petrov remained in Germany visiting as many aviation and instrument factories as possible; in his memoirs he mentions that he was able to visit a total of 219 "objects"! He had been given the personal task by Stalin to assess the production capacity of the German aircraft industry — "because even if we have signed the pact, Germany was and remains a vicious enemy. We must as soon as possible realize the German promise to sell us aircraft and engines. According to the agreement they must show us their entire aviation industry, and that is why you should try to estimate its potential. In case of war it is extremely important for us to know how many warplanes they are able to produce per day."

Petrov estimated this to be 60 to 70 aircraft daily, ie considerably higher than the Soviet capacity of 26 aircraft per day, and initially presented his estimation at the session of the Collegium of the People's Commissariat for Aviation Industry.

---

[11] 1899-1985; he became a Hero of the Soviet Union on 28 September 1934 after a record long distance flight, over 12.000 km in the ANT-25 special long-distance aircraft designed by A.N. Tupolev. During the war he commanded the 1 and 3 Air Armies, and from 1946 to 1949 he was Deputy Commander of the Dal'naya aviatsiya Long Range Air Force. Today LII bears the honorary name "imeni M.M.Gromova" (named after M.M.Gromov).

The newly-appointed Commissar Aleksandr I. Shakhurin[12] understood at once the importance of Petrov's information and asked for an immediate audience in the Kremlin.

After Petrov's short report Stalin asked a number of clarifying questions — such as how had he deduced the numbers? Stalin requested the calculations from the nervous Petrov and read the document while walking around in his office without saying a word.

As a result of Petrov's report immediate measures to increase the Soviet aircraft production capacity were taken, resulting in an output of 50 aircraft per day in June 1941, rising to over 70 aircraft by September 1941.

The publication in *Pravda* on 8 May 1940 of Petrov's promotion to Major-General made it, however, more difficult for him to move around in Germany as a civilian "aviation engineer" indicated in his passport. As a military man he now had two Gestapo shadows instead of the single one considered sufficient for an engineer. Petrov recalls that the Soviets were nevertheless able to test the German aircraft in good time before Hitler's attack, and distribute recognition leaflets in millions to the anti-aircraft, frontier guard, army and Air Force units (including the military flying schools). Petrov's group returned to the Soviet Union only a few days before the fateful 22 June 1941 by the last scheduled Berlin-Moscow train!

---

[12] 1904-75; appointed Commissar on 11 January 1940 — simultaneously with Yakovlev's promotion to Deputy Commissar. Shakhurin was forced to leave the top office of the aviation industry in connection with the conflict concerning the production of jet aircraft in 1946, and "heavily repressed" — see the section on Messerschmitt Me 262. After Stalin's death he was to get a ministerial post once again — now as Deputy Minister for Aircraft Production in 1953-57; ie reporting to his own wartime deputy P.V. Dementyev.

In 1943 a special exhibition of foreign and indigenous Soviet combat aircraft was established at the *Byuro Novoj Tekhniki* (Bureau of New Technology) of TsAGI, where Soviet engineers could make comparable studies of design solutions of various aircraft. Nothing is known about the ultimate fate of this unique aircraft collection. From left to right: A Messerschmitt Bf 109 G-2 ("15" of JG 53 – note the Ace of Spades emblem), an ex-RAF Bell Airacobra I (with engine and armament covers opened), a Curtiss P-40 "Kittyhawk" (engine cover open) and a "Tomahawk". The last aircraft in the left row is a Hawker Hurricane (of which only the tail is visible). On the right side a Petlyakov Pe-2 dive bomber and an Illushin Il-2 "Shturmovik" ground attack aircraft are to be seen.

In this photograph another two aircraft on the right row are visible: in the foreground a Yakovlev Yak-3 fighter with a Mikoyan MiG-3 fighter behind. The Hawker Hurricane in the back of the hall is clearly visible.

War Booty In The Great Fatherland War

The amount of booty taken by the Soviet forces during the war was tremendous, and contributed significantly to the Soviet war effort.

Shortly after the German attack a standing order to all Aviation Divisions was signed by Stalin, requiring that all shot-down and force-landed enemy aircraft be evacuated and delivered to the respective engineering groups for further handling.

Already on 29 July 1941 a permanent commission for reception of war-booty aircraft, led by Gen. M. Shishkin and including NII VVS engineers P. Rudintsev and G. Pechenko was formed.

TsAGI and the attached flight test institute LII were naturally given priority in examining captured German aircraft and equipment, and organized an efficient feed-back, primarily of aerodynamic and production technological information, to the Soviet design bureaux and aircraft factories, with NII VVS examining the captured hardware from a more comparative tactical-technical point of view. Thus from 1 to 6 February 1943 a joint scientific-technical conference with participants from TsAGI, TsIAM, OKBs and aircraft factories was organized at TsAGI with one of the main topics being "The German aircraft and their armament" presented by P. D. Samsonov. A permanent comparative exhibition of foreign (German and Lend-lease) and Soviet combat aircraft was also organized the *Byuro Novoj Tekhniki* (Bureau of New Technology) of TsAGI in 1943, with an extremely interesting collection of aircraft, including at least one Heinkel He 100, a Messerschmitt Bf 109 G-2, an ex-RAF Bell Airacobra I, a Curtiss P-40 "Kittyhawk", and "Tomahawk", a Hawker Hurricane, a Petlyakov Pe-2FT, an Ilyushin Il-2m3, a Mikoyan MiG-3 and a Yakovlev Yak-3. Unfortunately nothing is known of the subsequent fate of this unique aircraft collection.

Captured German aircraft of types already well-known to the Soviets were taken over by the engineering units of the fighting formations. For instance in the 16th Air Army commanded by Col.-Gen. Sergey I. Rudenko.[13] 446 aircraft were evacuated during September-December 1942, this number increasing to 685 for the period July-August 1943, rising to a total of 2371 aircraft evacuated during 1944. The aircraft were either repaired or dismantled for spares.

---

[13] 1904-90, HSU 19.8.1944, later CO of the Air-Borne Forces, Long-Range Air Force, 1st Deputy CO of the Soviet Air Force, etc.

The Soviet forces also started gradually to use captured German armament and bombs in large numbers, after demonstrations had been arranged for the distrustful Soviet crews, and the bombracks of Soviet aircraft had been modified to take the German bombs. According to Rudenko, after the Battle of Kursk in Summer 1943 as much as 20 per cent of the bombs dropped on the Germans were of their own production.

In 1944 over half a million German bombs were delivered to the Soviet Bomber Regiments by the war booty evacuation services.

At the end of June 1944 a big war booty exhibition was opened in the Culture Park (*Park Kultury*) in Moscow. The German aircraft exhibited included: Focke-Wulf Fw 58 "Weihe", Fw 189 "Uhu" and Fw 200 "Condor"; Heinkel He 111; Henschel Hs 129; Junkers Ju 87 and Ju 88; and Messerschmitt Bf 109F, Bf 109G-2 and Bf 110. All aircraft on display seem to be in very good condition in the published pictures, and most (if not all) had certainly been flight tested by the Russians.

From winter 1943 onwards a considerable number of aviators of the less reliable German allies, especially from the Slovak and Croatian Air Forces, defected to the Russian side. The recently published excellent *Slovak Airmen 1939–1945* by Jiří Rajlich and Jiří Sehnal gives a full picture of the Slovak defections. Thus, in spring 1943, two Avia B-534 and one Letov S-328 defected in the Ukraine, and in September 1943 three Slovak fighter pilots of 13.(Slovak)/JG52 based at Anapa defected with their Messerschmitt Bf 109-G4s. This symptom of low morale led to the withdrawal of the Slovak fighter Staffel from front-line duties.

As the Soviet forces approached Slovakia in late summer 1944, the number of defectors rose dramatically. Thus a He 111 and a Fw 58 carried representatives of the illegal Slovak National Council to Soviet-held territory from Tri Duby and Mokrad in Slovakia in the beginning of August 1944. Somewhat later a Junkers W34 and a Fw 189 defected eastwards, and on 31 August a virtual mass escape of 26 aircraft (seven S-328, six Fw 189, three B-534, two Bf 109-G-6, two Kl 35, one Bk-534, one Fi 156C, one Fw 58B, one Fw 44, one Praga E-39 and one Junkers W34) carrying 81 aviators from Isla in eastern Slovakia to Lvov took place.

Two days earlier, on 29 August 1944, a national uprising against the Germans and supporting the Allies had started in central Slovakia, with the insurgent air units being located at Tri Duby. This air force was to have received reinforcements from the ex-Slovak aircraft defected to the Soviet side, but as Tri Duby was captured by the Germans on 25 October 1944 only a few of the remaining airworthy insurgent aircraft escaped to the east.

During the closing stages of the Second World War the Soviet war booty began to pile up. For instance, — the First Belorussian Front reported the capture of 292 various aircraft plus a considerable number of transport gliders at the Posen area (now Poznan in western Poland) in February 1945; — a considerable number of factory-fresh "long-nosed" Focke-Wulf Fw 190D-9 fighters were captured intact at Marienburg, East Prussia (now Malbork, Poland), and so on.

When the Soviet forces entered Germany proper in spring 1945 the war booty naturally became even more interesting from the technical point of view: at Oranienburg, Dalgow, Damgarten, Tempelhof and other places a rich variety of such aircraft under development as the Me 163, Me 262, Ar 234, He 162, Do 335 and the "Mistel" etc. were captured.

The Soviet Union could even supply its allies with war-booty aircraft at the end of the war: in 1945 approximately 300 new Bf 109Fs and Fw 190s were found by Soviet troops at an airfield in Austria. The Chief Engineer of the Bulgarian Air Force Kabakchiev approached Gen. (Eng.) Aleksey L. Shepelev (Chief Engineer of 17th Air Army) asking whether the Bulgarian Air Force could be supplied with 50 of these aircraft. As this matter would require a political decision, Shepelev suggested that the Bulgarian Communist Leader and former Secretary General of Comintern Georgiy Dimitrov (1882-1949) should contact Stalin. This conversation between Dimitrov and Stalin obviously took place, as Shepelev soon got instructions to deliver a batch of the captured aircraft to the Bulgarian Air Force.

One of the last major applications of German war booty aircraft took place during the Aviation Day display on 18 August 1945, when a big number of ex-German Messerschmitts and Focke-Wulfs flew mock-combat against Soviet fighters, naturally now performing "the losing party". Maj. I. Piskunov made an especially impressive performance, simulating a force-landing of a Junkers Ju 388, shot down by Soviet fighters.

The Soviet Union received furthermore 20 ex-German aircraft from Sweden in autumn 1945, as the Russians claimed that German military personnel (including aircraft and other equipment) that had escaped from locations considered to be Soviet territory (ie Estonia, Latvia and Lithuania) should be returned to the USSR. This demand had especially tragic consequenses for the Baltic volunteers (considered to be Soviet citizens by the Soviet authorities) of the German armed forces, and caused considerable political problems in Sweden. Ultimately the Swedish government gave in to the Soviet demands, and about 3000 German soldiers (including 165 Balts) were returned to USSR — for further transportation to Gulag camps. Of the returned soldiers about 70 were air crews. The 18 German aircraft returned from Sweden to USSR (in flying condition or in parts) included four Fi 156s, four Fw 190s, three Bf 109s, two Fw 189s, and one each Bf 110, Bü 131, Ju 52, Do 24 and one Bü 181 (which was subsequently sold back to Sweden by the Soviet Embassy in Stockholm before transportation to USSR). In addition two Fw 156s were destroyed on the request of the Soviet inspecting commission in Sweden.

One of the Heinkel He 100 experimental fighters bought from Germany in 1940 was also exhibited at TsAGI.

A Focke-Wulf Fw 58 Weihe at the war booty exhibition in Moscow. The picture seems to have been taken in late autumn 1944, as the snow has already fallen.

A Messerschmitt Bf 109F at the war booty exhibition in Moscow. The picture seems to have been taken in late autumn of 1944, as the snow is already on the ground. Note the Heinkel He 111 and an unidentified twin-engined aircraft in the background on the ground!.

In late summer 1944 an attempt to assasinate Stalin "Operation Zeppelin" was carried out. On 6 September 1944, after several unsuccessful attempts a commando group including volunteer ex-prisoners of war was landed at Karmanovo (between Vyazma and Rzhev) approx 150 km west of Moscow by an Arado Ar 232B-05 (K1 + ZX, WNr 110017) of I./KG 200. The aircraft was damaged on landing. The commando group disguised as Soviet officer couriers ("Maj, Hero of the Soviet Union Tavrin, and the female "Jun.-Lt Shilova", were on the way to Moscow in a side-car motor cycle when caught at a road control point near Rzhev. All participants (including the six-man KG 200 crew) were probably captured and executed (or perished in Soviet camps).

In the spring of 1945 a batch of factory-fresh Focke-Wulf Fw 190D-9s were captured at Marienburg in East Prussia (now Malbork, Poland). The long-nosed Fw 190s were taken over by a Fighter Aviation Regiment of the VVS KBF (Air Force of the Baltic Fleet). Note the various aircraft in the background: a Douglas C-47, a Douglas A-20 Boston and a number of Yakovlev fighters can be identified on the original print.

The three-engined Savoia-Marchetti SM 82 used by Luftwaffe for various transport duties was also captured by Soviet forces. Note the Yakovlev Yak-6 and the Douglas C-47 in the background.

Italian Macchi C.200 Saetta fighters captured at Stalingrad, winter 1943.

Berlin-Gatow on 25 April 1945. A seemingly intact Fw 190A-8 ("17", WNr 170412) in the foreground, among a number of not so complete Fw 190s. Note the Soviet Yakovlev Yak-9 fighters and a Junkers Ju 87 Stuka in the background.

View of a captured Luftwaffe base in East Prussia in spring 1945. In the foreground a Messerschmitt Bf 109 with a typical spiral decoration of the propeller spinner. In the background a Yakovlev Yak-3 fighter "28" of the French Normandie-Niemen volunteer squadron (which formed part of the 303 IAD of the Red Air Force).

umber of serviceable
ulgarian Arado Ar 196s
e captured in 1944 in the
k Sea. Note the Swan
lem on the aircraft coded
096 in the foreground.

first Soviet rocket-fighter
tested by NII VVS
pilot Grigoriy Ya.
hchivandzhi, who crashed
lly on the seventh test-flight
March 1943.
page 113)

A Japanese Mitsubishi Ki-46 "Dinah" long-range reconnaissance aircraft captured during the brief campaign against Japan August 1945.

They never made it to the front . . . A German train loaded with aircraft components in Soviet hands.

Individual Aircraft Histories

Arado Ar 234B

After the war a number of serviceable Arado Ar 234B jet bombers were found by the Soviets at Damgarten (between Rostock and Stralsund). It was decided to ferry one of the twin-jet (Jumo 004 of 900 kp thrust) Ar 234Bs to NII VVS. A special testing group led by Col. Pyotr M. Stefanovskiy[14] — then head of the Test Flight Department of NII VVS, NII VVS Chief Engineer Izrail G. Rabkin and the test pilot Aleksei G. Kubyshkin flew to Berlin in the sole Soviet Curtiss C-46 Commando transport (ex USAF 43-47271, which had already been tested by Stefanovskiy), arriving on 26 April, 1946.

In Damgarten it was found that the Ar 234 had only one running turbo-jet engine. After the other engine had been changed (there was ample supply of Jumo 004s) it was decided to fly the aircraft to Rechlin (a distance of approx. 100 km or 60 miles), as the short runway at Damgarten did not allow take-off with full fuel load. The main runway at Rechlin was however damaged, and Kubyshkin was forced to land the Ar 234 on a nearby gravel runway. While approaching Rechlin one turbo-jet engine caught fire, and the undercarriage mechanism failed. Nevertheless, Kubyshkin succeeded in lowering the undercarriage manually, and stopped the aircraft by using the braking parachute, with one engine in flames! (The recent history of NII VVS gives somewhat different details of this accident: on his third flight with the Ar 234 Kubyshkin's task was to test the response of the engines to the throttle, which obviously resulted in overload and subsequent fire!)

After this narrow escape the Ar 234 was repaired and a number of flights were performed from Rechlin, with the take-off weight gradually increased to the maximum limit. This required a ground-run equal to two-thirds of the Rechlin available runway as the Ar 234 accelerated very slowly. The aircraft was inspected among others by Col-Gen Sergei I. Rudenko, C.O. of the 16th Air Army, who especially noted the easily exchangeable under-wing mounted turbo-jet engines — a design solution so far not applied by the Soviets.

At this stage it was, however, decided to refrain from ferrying the Ar 234 to Moscow as the unreliable engines would have required a number of prepared reserved landing strips *en route*. Stefanovskiy concludes his account of the testing of the Ar 234 noting that "except for the braking parachute and the ejectable fuel tanks there was nothing special with the aircraft".

---

[14] 1903-76, HSU 5.3.1948 as Maj-Gen, published his extremely interesting memoirs "*Trista neizvestnykh*" ("Three-hundred unknowns" – referring to the number of aircraft he tested!) in 1968, second edition printed in 1973. Stefanovskiy had test-flown a large number of foreign-made war booty and lend-lease aircraft.

A Blohm & Voss Bv 138 flying-boat (coded + D) was captured almost intact at Ventspils (Windau), Latvia in May 1945.

The Bv 138 sister ship "+ G" was badly damaged by artillery fire.

Blohm & Voss Bv 138

In October 1944 a Blohm & Voss Bv 138 flying-boat which had carried out reconnaissance flights over the White Sea was captured intact by the Soviet Navy. After having run out of fuel the German aircraft landed on the water near the Morzhovets Island at the mouth of the White Sea. It was detected first by Soviet radio intelligence and later visually by the crew of a Beriyev MBR-2 flying-boat. The German crew was picked up on 23 October 1944 by the hydrographical vessel *Mgla* (ex *Seemöwe*, 254 BRT) commanded by Captain 3rd Class I.Ye. Gorshkov of the White Sea Naval Flotilla.

Nothing is known of the possible testing and fate of this Bv 138 flying-boat.

A Bücker Bü 181 Bestmann trainer at the NII GVF (Research Institute of the Civil Aviation). Note the Douglas C-47 and the Junkers W 34 (?) in the background.

Bücker Bü 131 Jungmann

Three Bücker Bü 131 Jungmann trainers were delivered from Germany in 1940. They were extensively flown by LII test pilots, eg. Mark L. Gallaj (HSU 1.5.1957, who after his extensive test-pilot career acquired a Doctor's degree in aerodynamics, and later became a well-known author), Aleksei N. Grinchik and Igor I. Shelest, who performed advanced aerobatics, including prolonged inverted flight with the Jungmann. (The *Letno-issledovatel'skiy institut* had been founded at the beginning of 1940 on the base of the Flight Test Department of TsAGI.) The Bücker is also reported to have been flown in the NII VVS by the female test pilot Nina I. Rusakova.

In spring 1945 two fighter aces of the 152 Guards IAP (ex 270 IAP) Nikolay K. Shutt (HSU 4.2.1944, total score 55 victories) and Garri A. Merkviladze (HSU 27.6.1945, after 13 individual and 2 "group" victories; including one Me 262 jet) found a small German aircraft (a Jungmann or a Jungmeister?) at their ex-Luftwaffe forward base. The pilots immediately tried aerobatics with the German plane — without necessary formalities, nor informing the near-by Soviet anti-aircraft units, which immediately opened fire on the low-flying German aircraft! As a result of the complaints from the A-A regiment of the "hooliganism" of the "childish pilots", which could have cost the lives of the two aces, Shutt was grounded for some time by the C.O. of the 12 Guards IAD (ex 203 IAD) Maj.-Gen. K.G.Baranchuk.

One Bü 131, VT + AN, W.Nr. 4346, was flown to the Soviet Union via Turku, Finland, from Bromma, Sweden, on 27 August 1945. The aircraft had arrived at Malmö, Sweden from the *Flugzeugführerschule Warnemünde* on 1 May 1945.

Another Bücker Bü 181 Bestmann ("13") in flight in 1945.

Bücker Bü 133 Jungmeister

Three Bücker Bü 133 Jungmeister single-seat aerobatic trainers were delivered from Germany in 1940. A number of LII test-pilots including Igor I. Shelest, Viktor L. Rastorguyev, Aleksey N. Grinchik and Sergey N. Anokhin (HSU 3.2.1953) are known to have performed aerobatics with the Jungmeister.

Dornier Do 24

A Dornier Do 24 flying-boat is known to have been used by *Polarnaya Aviatsiya* after the war and flown by Matvey I. Kozlov and others. The origin of this (or these?) aircraft is not known. It could have been 5W + BU (W.Nr. 42) of *Seenotstaffel 50*, which arrived in Trelleborg, Sweden, from Ventspils (Windau) in Latvia with 37 (!) refugees on board on 9 May 1945. This aircraft was flown to the Soviet Union as requested on 14 August 1945 by a Russian transfer crew.

A three-engined Dornier Do 24 flying-boat. Note the former location of the swastika on the tail, clearly overpainted with a red star! The Do 24 is known to have been used in the Soviet Arctic regions for some time after the war.

Dornier Do 17/215

Two Dornier Do 17Zs (with export designation Do 215 B-3; the different designations applied have caused some confusion among Soviet authors) were delivered from Germany in 1940, and subsequently extensively test-flown at LII (the leading test-pilot being Pavel F. Mushtayev; also flown by Mark L. Gallaj) and at NII VVS.

Even if they were completely different aircraft, the specialists of NII VVS noticed many common characteristics (but differing from the Soviet design principles!) of the Do 215 and of the simultaneously tested Ju 88. Both were all-metal aircraft, flown by a four-member crew in a common cockpit (which enabled the crew members to easily assist each other), armed with three MG-15 machine guns etc. Both bombers could reliably be flown with only one engine (which the contemporary Soviet bombers, the Tupolev SB and Ilyushin DB-3 were unable to do).

The Soviets also noted the great importance laid on use of standardized details facilitating series production, and especially the ability of the aircraft to stand battle damage (separated, hermetic fuel tanks with double fuel tubes etc). The Do 215 could carry 1000 kg bombs internally in the bomber version, or alternatively take an additional 900 litres of fuel in the recce version (does this remark indicate that one bomber and one recce Do 215 variant were delivered to the USSR?).

The Do 215 climbed very fast: with a flight weight of 8621 kg, the Do 215B climbed to 5000 m in 10.8 minutes.

In summer 1941 it was decided to establish a special reconnaissance unit using the German aircraft delivered one year previously: three (?) Dornier Do 215s, three (?) Junkers Ju 88s, three Messerschmitt Bf 110s and three Bf 109s — i.e. a total of 12 aircraft. This unit was commanded by a veteran from the Spanish Civil War, the NII VSS test-pilot Maj. Valentin I. Khomyakov (HSU 8.1.1980) with another NII VVS test-pilot Fyodor F. Opadchiy (HSU 7.2.1957) as flying instructor. The crews of this special unit consisted of a number of Spanish pilots who had arrived in the Soviet Union after the civil war. The training took place at a remote airfield in the Urals region. Among the Spanish pilots who flew the Do 215 were Antonio Arias (who erroneously calls it "Do 117" in his memoirs published in Minsk in 1988) with Vicente Beltram as co-pilot.

The planned use of this unit for clandestine reconnaissance flights over the German rear areas was however not realized, and the Spanish pilots were transferred to the *Vojska protivo-vozdushnoy oborony* (Air Defence forces) in Moscow, arriving there on 7 November. Meanwhile Opadchiy was badly injured in an accident while flying a Junkers Ju 88 (*see* section on this aircraft for details).

At least one of the Do 215 aircraft was however used for the clandestine recce tasks planned for the Spanish pilots — but piloted by Valentin P. Sokolov of the *2 aviatsionnyy polk dal'ney razvedki* (Long distance recconnaissance regiment), subsequently transformed into 47 Guards DRAP on 8 February 1943). Sokolov (HSU 15.5.1946) even flew with the Do 17 over Berlin at least twice in late autumn 1941, being one of the first Soviet pilots to fly over the German capital.

The *Polarnaya Aviatsiya* pilot Valentin I. Akkuratov (later to become a well-known pilot in the Long-Range Air Force ADD, and subsequently a popular writer) describes a strange encounter with a Dornier Do 17 (possibly one of the Do 215 B-3s delivered from Germany?) *en route* to Kazan (800 km behind the front lines) in November 1941. The PS-84 (licence-built DC-3) crew consisting of Georgi K. Orlov and Akkuratov were given the special task of delivering important mail from Moscow to Sevastopol via Kazan, Krasnodar and Novorossiysk. During the flight to Kazan the navigator Sergei Namestikov noticed a Do 17 with the German black crosses (!) clearly visible, closing in on the Soviet transport aircraft! The Soviet crew decided to "wait and see", not letting the strange German aircraft closer than 50m. The lone German did not open fire but seemed only to follow in the same direction. On approaching Kazan the German aircraft disappeared out of sight, but when Orlov landed at the airport of the Kazan Aircraft Factory (GAZ No. 22) the Dornier Do 17 was already parked there. The Soviet crew of the ex-German aircraft smiled and was grateful for the guidance — they had the task of ferrying the captured aircraft to the Aircraft Factory No. 22, with the radio and navigational instruments out of order! No deviation from the predetermined route was possible — this would have caused immediate alert of the PVO units with fateful consequences. When forced-landing seemed to be the only option left for the ferry crew, the *Polarnyaya Aviatsiya* aircraft was detected, and the Dornier Do 17 crew decided to follow the PS-84, hoping that the Polar aviators were heading for Kazan. No further information is given of this mysterious ex-German bomber by Akkuratov.

Dornier Do 217

According to the history of TsAGI the Dornier Do 217 (here again erroneously called "Do 117") was also delivered from Germany in 1940. I.F. Petrov (Director of TsAGI) states however that the Soviet specialists were "fortunate" to refuse to buy the Do 217 (Do 17?), as it was not to have extensive operational use in the Luftwaffe. No other known sources mentioned the use of this aircraft type in the Soviet Union. (The Do 17 Z/Do 215 B-3 is presumably meant by the references to Do 117/217).

Dornier Do 335

A "strange-looking aircraft with one propeller in the nose and another in the rear, and antennas along the wings" was found by two officers of the 812 IAP, Major Yegor Ye. Ankudinov (deputy regiment CO; HSU 15.5.1946 with a total of 15 victories) and Capt. Aleksandr T. Tishshenko (regimental shturman (navigator); HSU 15.5.1946 with a total of 16 individual and 1 shared air victory), while inspecting a hangar at Oranienburg in April 1945. No other traces of the unmistakably well described Do 335 have so far been found in the Soviet literature.

Fieseler Fi 156 Storch

Two Fieseler Fi 156 Storch were delivered from Germany in 1940. General Ernst Udet offered the leader of the Soviet military-industrial delegation Ivan F. Tevosyan (People's Commissar for Shipbuilding Industry) a flight in a Storch when he was touring the German industry in late 1939. According to the Yakovlev memoirs this aircraft was subsequently presented to the Soviet delegation as a gift by Reichsmarschall Hermann Göring.[15]

One of the Storchs was subsequently employed as a courier aircraft by NII VVS and flown by the test-pilots Pyotr M. Stefanovskiy, Aleksandr S. Nikolayev, Stepan P. Suprun and others while the other one was used as a pattern aircraft by Yakovlev's Deputy Oleg K. Antonov who was given the task of designing a "similar" (analog) Russian aircraft. Antonov performed the task quickly, and the OKA-38 *Aist* (*OKA* after the initials of Antonov, *Aist* is Russian for Storch!) prototype passed the State Acceptance Tests successfully after only 8 months. The OKA-38 was powered by a 220 hp MV-6 engine, and used a wing

---

[15] Fi 156 is reported to have already been delivered to Moscow via Kaunas on 6 October 1939. This aircraft was coded D-IXWO, which implies that Göring gave his present immediately after the signing of the non-aggression pact (ie. before the visit of Tevosyan's delegation).

Oleg Antonov designed a copy of the Fieseler Storch courier aircraft delivered from Germany in 1940. Antonov's aircraft was designated OKA-38 Aist (Storch) and powered by a 220 hp MV-6 engine (note the different shape of the nose of the aircraft compared to German Storch with Argus AS 10 engine). The Aist was ready for series production at Factory No 465 in Kaunas, Lithuania when the German forces attacked on 22 June 1941.

profile called R-II, designed by the Soviet aerodynamicist P.P. Krasil'shchikov. The series production of the courier aircraft SS-1 (SS for *Samolet Svyazi* or Courier Aircraft, the military designation of the OKA-38 was set up in Aircraft Factory No. 465 at Kaunas (Lithuania). The production of an ambulance version designated SS-2 was also prepared. The town of Kaunas and Factory No. 465 were however to be quickly overrun by the German forces on 22 June 1941, and as a result the *Aist* was destined never to be produced in the Soviet Union.

During the war a number of serviceable Storchs were captured on different sections of the German-Soviet front and were apparently quite popular as courier aircraft in the Soviet Air Force. Maj-Gen Yevgeniy Ya. Savitskiy[16] (C.O. 205 IAD) used a Storch late December 1942 when he was suddenly summoned to Moscow from the Stalingrad area in extremely unfavourable weather conditions. The CO of the Soviet Air Force Col-Gen Aleksandr A. Novikov and Gen A.V. Nikitin of the Air Force HQ thought it was very childish of Savitskiy to use a German courier aircraft — a commander in his position should have known better!

---

[16] 1910- , commanded 205 IAD, 3 IAK RVGK or the 3rd Fighter Aviation Corps of the Reserve of the Supreme Command. He scored a total of 22 individual and two shared victories, and was twice made an HSU; on 11 May 1944 and 2 June 1945. After the war he served as Deputy CO of the Air-Defence Forces. His daughter Svetlana Savitskaya became the second female cosmonaut, performing a space flight on board the Soyuz T-7/Salyut-7 spacecraft from 19 to 27 August 1982 after winning the world championship in aerobatics in 1970 and establishing 18 world records in aviation. Svetlana flew in space for the second time from 17 to 29 July 1984, and like her father was twice made a Hero of the Soviet Union; on 27 August 1982 and 29 July 1984 respectively.

On 12-13 May 1945 Savitskiy was again using an Fi 156, when he flew from Berlin to Moscow with Maj. L. Novikov as pilot for an operation on his left leg, inflamed by a large number of shell splinters.

The commissar of the 812 IAP, Maj. Timofej Ye. Pasynok also used a Storch found at the former Luftwaffe base at Sokhachev in January 1945 as his personal hack after he was prohibited from flying the Soviet-built fighters of the regiment for medical reasons.

The well-known Soviet Airacobra-ace, twice Hero of the Soviet Union, Sultan Amet-Khan,[17] intercepted a Storch-courier aircraft which had lost its orientation en route from Constanta in Romania to Yevpatoria in Crimea and forced it to land at Kiligeyskiye Khutora in autumn 1943. On the following day the Storch was flown by Sultan Amet-Khan to the main base of his regiment at Chaplinka with the captured German pilot as passenger.

At least two cases are known where Soviet POWs escaped in Storchs stolen from Luftwaffe bases. On August 11 1943 Nikolay K. Loshakov (of the

A captured battle-damaged Fieseler Fi 156 Storch at a Soviet AF base. Note other ex-German aircraft in the background (from left to right): a Focke-Wulf Fw 58 Weihe, a Focke-Wulf Fw 189 Uhu and a Junkers W 34.

14 Guards IAP, which had been transformed from the 7 IAP of the 13th Air Army on 7 March 1942) escaped from Ostrov with Ivan A. Denisyuk as passenger, landing at Malaya Vishegra in the Novgorod area after a flight of 3 hours in the red-painted Storch courier aircraft of the Commandant of the Luftwaffe base at Orlov, Alois Moyzisch. Loshakov had been shot down on 27 May 1943 near Sinyavino on the Leningrad front. (No decorations of Loshakov are known, as he was obviously suspected of being a German agent! According to a Soviet documentary novel, one of the German officers held responsible for the escape of

---

[17] 9 Guards IAP, which had been transformed from 69 IAP on 7 March 1942. Amet-Khan got his HSU awards on 24 August 1943 and 29 June 1945. He scored a total of 30 personal and 19 shared victories. After the war he became a test-pilot, and was killed when testing a new prototype on 1 February 1971.

One of many Storchs captured by the Soviets.

Several Storchs were captured intact by the Soviet forces, and they were rather popular as courier aircraft among VVS personnel. In the picture is U2 + AB of I./NAGr 5, which operated in the Baltic area in 1944-45 (note another captured Storch DH + ML in the background)

Loshakov, the fighter-pilot Gustav Heuler deserted to the Soviets in September 1943, landing with his Fw 190 at a Soviet AF base in the Leningrad area.)

On 4 October, 1943 the ADD pilot Arkadiy Kovyazin escaped from Riga-Spilve in a Storch, landing at Lipovka (50 km NW Rzhev). He had made a forced landing behind the German lines in 1941, and was imprisoned in the POW camp No. 350 in Riga. His unit was the 212 ODAP DD which had meanwhile been transformed into 748 AP DD, and subsequently into 12 Guards AP DD on 18 August 1942. (After "many years" Kovyazin was decorated with the Order of Lenin.)

In the winter of 1944-45 a Storch was used as a courier aircraft by 122 IAP (subordinated to 331 IAD) in Hungary.

Finally four Storchs which had escaped to Sweden from Latvia in early May 1945, were flown to the Soviet Union via Turku, Finland on 27 August 1945: PV + ZZ (of *14./Fl.Verb.G. 2*, WNr 5323; landed in Sweden on 1 May 1945) KC + LJ (WNr 5044; landed in Sweden on 1 May 1945) U2 + OB (of *Stab I./NAGr 5*; arrived in Sweden 9 May 1945) and KP + GI (landed in Sweden 9 May 1945).

Focke-Wulf Fw 58 Weihe

Three Focke-Wulf Fw 58 Weihe training/communications aircraft were bought from Germany in 1940, and tested by the Soviet Union, flown among others by Igor I. Shelest at LII). One Fw 58B-2 (WNr 2754, registration D-OXWR) had been delivered in May 1940.

One Fw 58 Weihe was displayed at the war-booty exhibition in Moscow in summer 1943.

Focke-Wulf Fw 189 Uhu

According to L.L. Kerber a Focke-Wulf Fw 189 Uhu (which was called *"Rama"* by the Soviets because of its twin-boom configuration) was delivered to NII VVS in 1940. However, there is no confirmation from other authors — and it could well be that Kerber is mistaken and that he is in fact referring to the Focke-Wulf Fw 58 Weihe (which was delivered). Photographs of an Fw 189 with "red stars", presumably taken at NII VVS (but at an unknown date!) do however exist.

At NII VVS the excellent radio equipment (the FuG-17 VHF radio) was especially noted.

The female NII VVS test pilot Nina I. Rusakova is reported to have tested a "Focke-Wulf" aircraft — the subtype is unfortunately not mentioned in the NII VVS history!

An Fw 189 Uhu was displayed at the war-booty exhibition in Moscow in summer 1943.

Two Fw 189s were flown to Tallinn from Sweden on 29 August 1945. These two aircraft (U2 + ZB, WNr 2274 and U2 +RB, WNr 125345) of *Stab I./NAGr 5* had arrived in Bulltofta from Latvia on 8 May 1945. The German crew were also handed over to the Soviet authorities.

Children playing by a pair of no-more-airworthy Focke-Wulf Fw 189 Uhus of Stab I/NAGr 5 in Estonia in late summer 1945. The codes U2 + XB and U2 + ZB can be recognized. These two aircraft had arrived at Bulltofta, Sweden on 8 May, 1945 with defecting Luftwaffe personnel from Latvia. According to the Swedish-Soviet agreement they were handed over to the Soviet Union at Bromma on 28 August 1945 and flown to Tallinn the following day.

A Focke-Wulf Fw 189
Uhu at NII VVS. Note that
the tail rudder seems to
come from another
aircraft.

Focke-Wulf Fw 190

When the Focke-Wulf Fw 190 began to appear in larger numbers on the Eastern Front in 1942-43 the Red Air Force command considered it extremely important to capture intact examples of this potent — until then unknown — fighter for evaluation by Soviet specialists.

The CO of the 13 Guards IAD (ex-294 IAD), Maj-Gen Anton D. Yakimenko (HSU 29.8.39) is obviously mistaken in his memoirs when he states seeing an Fw 190 among other German aircraft — the Me 109s, He 111s, "He 113s" and Ju 88s in a "closed hangar" (ie obviously at NII VVS) in February 1941. No other sources indicate deliveries of any Fw 190s, which would have virtually been impossible at that early date: The TsAGI director I.F. Petrov relates however that the Soviet specialists "fortunately" refused to buy the Fw 190 (in 1940!) as it was to have very limited use at the front, while the People's Commissar A.S. Shakhurin states that the Germans did not tell a word about the existence of the Fw 190 prototypes to the visiting Soviet specialists. Shakhurin's version is certainly correct. That the Soviets obviously did believe that they had purchased the prototype of another German fighter is proved by the frequent references to "He 113" fighters in the Soviet reminiscence literature — (eg note the citation above from the memoirs of Yakimenko!). The "He 113" was in fact a German propaganda hoax; the Heinkel factory defence squadron of He 100 fighters was widely publicised in spurious operational markings and described the "He 113").

This Focke-Wulf Fw 190A-4 (WNr 2310) was the first serviceable "190" captured by the Soviet forces on 13 January 1943, when *Uffz* Helmut Brandt 2./JG 54 made a forced landing on the ice of the south-eastern shore of Lake Ladoga. The aircraft was overhauled at the *1. Remontnaya Baza* (Repair Depot) in Leningrad. As the propeller had been damaged in the landing, it is said to have been replaced by an airscrew from a Junkers Ju 87!

A new airscrew and underbelly coating have already been fitted to the Fw 190 "2". Note the clearly visible *"Grünherz"* insignia of JG 54 and the Nürnberg city coat of arms emblem of I./JG 54. An Ilyshin Il-2 *"Shturmovik"* is seen in the background.

The first Fw 190 captured intact was obviously an A-4 of 2./JG 54 (WNr 2310, piloted by *Uffz* Helmut Brandt) which made a forced landing on the ice of Lake Ladoga east of Schlüsselburg on 13 January 1943 after a combat with Capt Sergei G. Litavrin, Sen-Ltns Sergei V. Demenkov, Grigori I. Bogomazov and A.I. Morozov of the 158 IAD PVO (to become 103 Guards IAP on 7 July 1943). The Soviet pilots shot down one of the two Fw 190s, while the other force-landed on the ice of the frozen lake. This German Fw 190-pilot was able to escape to the coastline held by German forces. The aircraft was evacuated by Soviet troops at night and transported to the Komendantskiy naval air force base near Leningrad, where it was dismantled and examined in detail. Pilots from neighbouring units (eg the 3 Guards IAP of VVS KBF; ex-5 IAP, awarded "Guards" status on 18 January 1942) were invited to study the captured aircraft. As the propeller had been damaged in the landing it is said to have been replaced by an airscrew from a Junkers Ju 87 at the *1. Remontnaya Baza* (Repair Depot) in Leningrad. After the local study the Fw 190A-4 was transferred to TsAGI for detailed examination and testing. Responsible test pilot was Yuriy A. Antipov (HSU 9.9.1957), who recorded a max. speed of 610 km/h at 6000m, and a one-second fire burst of 4.93 kg. Antipov noted especially the automatic engine control, superior equipment and structural strength. However, the aircraft was considered too heavy, which impaired its manoeuvrability.

In 1944 it was displayed at the comparative exhibition of foreign and Soviet aircraft at TsAGI.

Litavrin was made a Hero of the Soviet Union on 28 January 1943 for capturing the Fw 190, while Demenkov and Bogomazov were to get this award later on 28 September 1943, and 2 October 1943 respectively.

Another belly-landed Fw 190A-4 (WNr 5790, "Yellow 4") of JG 54 (note the *Grünherz* emblem), piloted by *Oberleutnant* Günther Götze who did not return on 1 February 1943.

53

Another Fw 190 made a forced landing in winter 1943 at the North-Western Front covered by the 6th Air Army commanded by Maj-Gen Fyodor P. Polynin (already an HSU on 14 November 1938 as a volunteer pilot in China); a more detailed location is unfortunately not given. The Inspector of the VVS Headquarters, Col. N.G. Seleznev arrived from Moscow to test it. After two days of meticulous inspection of the aircraft on the ground he made the first flight — and found the Fw 190 heavy in the aerobatics. In his opinion, the new Soviet fighters were more manoeuvrable. Seleznev recommended to attack the Fw 190 from above or from underneath where it was vulnerable. Among the other deficiencies noted by him were poor forward vision, and the unshielded fuel tank which could be easily set on fire. On explicit Stavka orders the aircraft was later ferried to Moscow for further investigation by Seleznev.

An Fw 190 was also captured intact on the Southern Front in summer 1943 by Ltn Semejko of the 814 IAP (to become 106 Guards IAP on 25 August 1943). Semejko was leading a group of four Yaks when two Fw 190s were encountered. One Focke-Wulf fighter was shot down, and the other was surrounded by the Soviet pilots in a "pincer" formation, and forced to land at a Soviet base. This Fw 190 is said to have been piloted by a German flying-instructor.

One of the German officers held responsible for the escape of Nikolai Loshakov in an Fi 156 Storch from Ostrov on 11 August 1943, the fighter-pilot Gustav Heuler deserted to the Soviets in September 1943, landing with his Fw 190 at a Soviet AF base in the Leningrad area (*see* pages 47-48).

This Fw 190A-4 (WNr 5772) probably did not fly again. The aircraft was flown by *Feldwebel* Bremer (1./JG 54) who crash-landed at Krasnogorye on 13 July 1943.

An Fw 190A-8 (?) of an unknown *Luftwaffe* unit captured by the Soviets in obviously serviceable condition.

Luftwaffe wreckage captured at the Khersonnes AF base in the Crimea on 12 May 1944. The foremost tailpiece belonged to Fw 190, WNr 190079, and the aircraft just behind is WNr 160749 (?). Note the insignia of the *Gruppen-Kommandeur* of II. Gruppe — was this the former aircraft of Maj. Heinz Frank, *Gruppen-Kommandeur* of II./SG 2 "Immelmann"?)

A number of Focke-Wulf Fw 190s were test-flown by Maj-Gen Georgi N. Zaharov (*see* page 9), and extensively tested by the experienced NII VVS and LII test-pilots.

Yuri A. Antipov was the responsible test-pilot at NII VVS for the Fw 190A-8 (he also tested the Fw 190A-4 as mentioned above and Fw 190A-5 versions). Other test-pilots flying the Focke-Wulf fighter included Vasili Ye. Golofastov of NII VVS, and the LII test-pilots Viktor L. Rastorguyev (killed on 16 August 1945 in the hybrid Yak-3RD with a liquid-fuel rocket 'booster' motor), Aleksi I. Grinchik and Mark L. Gallaj.

At NII VVS the Fw 190A-4 was found to be inferior to the new Soviet fighters (Yakovlev Yak-1 and Yak-7B, and especially the Lavochkin La-5) in vertical manoeuvres, but more or less equal in horizontal movements. The Soviet test pilots also noted that the Fw 190 was rather heavy in controls compared to the extremely manoeuvrable light-weight Soviet fighters.

Antipov performed a mock-combat in the Fw 190 against Yak-1s piloted by the test-pilots Leonid M. Kuvshinov and Vasili G. Ivanov (both Kuvshinov and Ivanov were made HSU on 9.9.1957): He also demonstrated the Fw 190 to a number of fighter regiments of 2nd and 4th Air Armies, commanded by Lt-Gen Semyon A. Krasovskiy and Lt-Gen Konstantin A. Vershinin respectively.

A Focke-Wulf Fw 190A-4 at NII VVS. — Note that the fuselage is devoid of red stars insignia.

Another Focke-Wulf Fw 190A-4 at NII VVS. Note the remains of the I./JG 54 "Nürnberg" emblem at the nose. Is this the aircraft of *Uffz* Helmut Brandt of 2./JG 54 which was evacuated from Lake Ladoga in January 1943?

Both the cannon-equipped Fw 190A-8/R6 and the "enlightened" Fw 190A-8 (WNr 580967) subtypes were tested at the NII VVS. The MK-108 cannon-equipped version had an impressive one-second fire burst of 9.74 kg, but was considered to be primarily intended for ground-attacks and thus no match for the new Soviet dogfighters. The new "light-weight" A-8 had a fuel capacity of only 393 kg, and an armament of two heavy machine-guns and two 20mm Mauser cannons, giving a one-second fire burst of 3.44 kg. A max. speed of 542 km/h at ground level, and 642 km/h at 6,500m was recorded. The time to climb to 500 m was 5.4 min with a take-off weight of 3,986 kg. However, repeated mock-combat where the Fw 190A-8 was flown by a big number of NII VVS pilots (in addition to Antipov, it was also flown by I.M. Dzyuba — HSU 21.7.1942 as squadron C.O. of 12 IAP, A. Kubyshkin, L.M. Kuvshinov, A. Proshakov and V.P. Khomyakov — HSU 8.1.1980) against the latest Soviet fighters (Yak-3, Yak-9U and the La-7) showed unanimously that the times of German fighter supremacy were gone.

Not even the long-nose Fw190D-9 (powered by the liquid-cooled Jumo 213A) tested at the NII VVS two months later could change the above-mentioned conclusion. V. Golofastov recorded a max. speed of 624 km/h at 5000 m altitude, climbing to 5000 m in 5.6 minutes with a take-off weight of 4,197 kg. The Yak-3 had decidedly better performance up to an altitude of 5,500m.

In the spring of 1945 a batch of factory-fresh Focke-Wulf Fw 190D-9s were captured at Marienburg in East Prussia (now Malbork, Poland). (See page 34 for another picture of these aircraft!)

A Focke-Wulf Fw 190D-9 being tested at NII VVS.

In March 1945 the 2 Guards IAP of 322 IAD (ex-526 IAP, which had already achieved the Guards status on 6 December 1941 as one of the first aviation regiments) was located at Zarau near a former Focke-Wulf factory. A large number of "long-nosed Focke-Wulfs" (Fw 190 D-9s?) were found on the factory grounds. The "*Dora*" however was not flown by the Soviet pilots "as the La-7 was a better aircraft" according to the CO of the 322 IAD, Gen. Aleksandr F. Semenov (HSU after the Soviet-Finnish Winter War 21.3.1940). The war booty aircraft were used for gun-sighting and identification training on the ground by the pilots of the 322 IAD — with the engineers turning the German fighters to different angles at various distances (200, 400 and 600m).

On 27 April, 1945 an Fw 190 flown by the German pilot Wagner (taking off for his first and last solo flight from Hagenow) was forced down at the base of the 55 Guards IAP (ex-581 IAP, promoted to a "Guards" regiment on 31 January 1943) in the Berlin area.

In the spring of 1945 several German reports indicated encounters with Fw 190s marked "with red stars":

On 26 March 1945 a group of four Heinkel He 111 and four Dornier Do 217 bombers of KG 200 tried to destroy the bridges over the Oder river at Göritz-Mitte and Neurathstock without success. An Fw 190 "with a Soviet star" was encountered among the attacking Soviet fighters.

On 26 April 1945 Luftflotte 6 reported shooting down an Fw 190 with red *Balkenkreuz* (!) under its wings, a "Soviet star" on the fuselage and black-white-red cockade on the tail. Insignia was verified through downing. The pilot — probably German — was killed. (*See* appendix 3 for a discussion on this theme.)

Four Fw 190s which had escaped to Sweden on 8 May 1945 (WNr 739137 of 1./JG 54, WNr 682790 of 5./JG 54, WNr 931484 and 584205 of III./SG 3) were dismantled and delivered to the USSR on 8 November 1945.

Focke-Wulf Fw 200 Condor
The Russians got their first external view of the Fw 200 when Foreign Minister von Ribbentrop flew to Moscow on 23 August 1939 for his meeting with Stalin and Molotov. The aircraft used by the German foreign minister was D-ACVH "*Grenzmark*" (WNr 3098, of sub-type Fw 200A-0), piloted by Hitler's personal pilot Hans Baur, who has described the great interest the Russian ground personnel showed in his aircraft during its stay at the Moscow Central Airport.

A Focke-Wulf Fw 200G Condor which was captured intact at Stalingrad early 1943 was tested at NII VVS. The Soviet test-pilots noted the poor performance of the aircraft (max. speed only 387 km/h at 4,200m, and bombload only 1000 kg at a take-off weight of 20 tons). As the aircraft was lacking armour protection and had only very weak defensive armament, it could not even be used practically as a nocturnal or strategic bomber. The Soviet Pe-8 (not to speak of the American B-17 "Flying Fortress") was considered to be superior in all respects. The Condor was displayed at the war-booty exhibition in Moscow June 1943.

A Focke-Wulf Fw 200C-4 at NII VVS. Note the earth globe emblem of KG 40, and the victory sign (one transport ship) on the tail. On the original print a multitude of various aircraft can be identified in the background: several Douglas C-47s, a Petlaykov Pe-8 four-engined bomber, a number of Polikarpov I-16 fighters and others.

In spring 1945 a number of Fw 200 Condors were captured in the Berlin area. The *Polarnaya Aviatsiya* pilot Mikhail A. Titlov (HSU 29.8.1955) was ordered to ferry a Condor to Moscow after two familiarization flights. The long-distance Condor was to be used in the Soviet far north regions, carrying out ice surveillance for the Arctic shipping routes. Titlov piloted the Condor for three months in 1946, flying up to 20 (!) hours a day. On the last flight from Khatanga to Moscow on 13 December, 1946 he had to force-land the civil-registered Condor (CCCP N-400) at Baydaratskaya Guba (69° 20' N, 67° 30' E) after the engines stopped one after another. The crew and passengers (a total of 21 persons) were subsequently rescued by a Douglas C-47 piloted by N.L. Syrokvasha and Valentin I. Akkuratov, who made a successful landing on the ice in the vicinity of Titlov's Condor. (For a picture of CCCP N-400, *see* page 16.)

Gotha Go 145

A Latvian pilot, J. Kirsteins of the night ground attack unit *NSGr 12* (the personnel being Latvian volunteers) defected to the advancing Soviet forces in Lithuania in a Gotha Go 145 on 24 July 1944.

This aircraft was later used by two Latvian pilots of the Soviet Air Force, Sen-Lt Nikolajs Vulfs and Lt Pavels Elvins (of the 1st Latvian NBAP) for a special task over German-occupied Latvia on 22 August 1944. The operation involved dropping an open letter from the imprisoned *General-Feldmarschall* Friedrich Paulus addressed to *Feldmarschall* Ferdinand Schörner (CO of *Armeegruppe Nord*), urging him to honorably capitulate.

Vulfs took off from Dekshnary (near Lubana in eastern Latvia) with message dropping points at Petreube, Pabazhi and Malpils, a total flight distance of 400 km, duration 2.5 hours at an altitude of only 10-15 m. Because of secrecy precautions the Soviet Air Defence units were not informed and, as the aircraft was obviously flying with German insignia, the Gotha Go 145 was fired on by various Soviet PVO anti-aircraft artillery units on its return flight (a total of 27 hits were counted) but Vulfs was able to reach his base and land successfully.

He was to encounter another incident when ferrying the Gotha Go 145 to the war booty exhibition at Minsk. When landing at Vilnius, Lithuania, for refuelling he was arrested suspected of being a German agent flying a German aircraft, and as a Latvian-speaking Russian with a heavy accent. Only after his identity had been positively established was he given permission to continue the flight to Minsk. Vulfs and Elvins were later decorated with the Order of the Red Banner for their special mission.

A Gotha Go 145 biplane in Soviet hands. Note the bomb racks under the wings, and that all identification insignia have been obliterated. Could this be the aircraft used by Sen-Lt Nikolajs Vulfs for his clandestine propaganda leaflet dropping operations over Latvia in August 1944?

This incident shows very clearly how the loyalties of the Latvian airmen were divided, with Latvian national fighting units existing both in the Luftwaffe and in the Red Air Force.

As in Estonia after the Soviet occupation in June 1940 the former Latvian Army was reorganised into the 24th Territorial Corps of the Red Army, with the Latvian Army Air Force correspondingly transferred into the Detached Aviation Squadron of the 24th Corps. This unit equipped with obsolete Belgian SV-5 aircraft practically ceased to exist on 14 July 1941, as no aircraft were serviceable and the personnel was dispersed.

On 20 January 1943 the General Staff of the Red Army however gave permission to establish the 24th Detached Latvian Aviation Escadrille, which was subsequently transformed into a regiment, the 1st Latvian NBAP (subordinated to 242 NBAD) commanded by Maj. Kârlis A. Kirss. Except for the well-known French volunteer *"Normandie-Niemen"* regiment the 1st Latvian NBAP was the only national unit of the VVS.

Practically at the same time, on the other side of the front lines, *Luftflotte 1* decided in September 1943 to organize an aviation school for Estonian and Latvian volunteers named *"Ergänzungs-Nachtschlachtgruppe Ostland"* near Liepaja in Courland, Latvia. This unit gradually became *Nachtschlachtgruppe 12* (*NSGr* 12) which was disbanded on 7 October 1944. (For details on these Latvian AF units in VVS and Luftwaffe, *see* Appendix 2.2.)

Gotha Go 242

In 1944 a Gotha Go 242 transport glider was evacuated from Heunau to Moscow by Adam Dabakhov and Grigori S. Malinovskiy as co-pilot. They flew out to Heunau, which had just been captured by Soviet forces, in two Polikarpov Po-2s. The Heunau airfield (called the "cemetery of gliders" by Soviet pilots) was full of damaged Gotha Go 242s, of which the best example was chosen for ferrying.

The Go 242 was towed by an elderly four-engined Tupolev TB-3 bomber piloted by Sen-Lt Pavel Yeremeyev. When the TB-3-Go 242 combination was about to take off the airstrip came under German fire. Soon after take-off it became necessary to disengage the Go 242 because of heavy vibrations at a height of only 100 m. Fortunately a Soviet frontal airstrip was directly ahead, and Dabakhov managed to land the glider successfully. At this airstrip a Douglas C-47 piloted by the former glider-pilot Abrosimov was available and the new combination took off for Moscow. Near Mogilev the weather deteriorated, and Abrosimov tried to underfly the clouds, but was forced to enter the fog. Dabakhov soon lost sight of the towing C-47 in the dense-fog — he could only see 5-6 m in front of him, with the length of the towing rope being 60 m. Nevertheless, after several risky, blind manoeuvres the party was able to land at the destination.

Heinkel He 100

The Heinkel He 100 experimental fighter (temporary holder of the absolute speed

The Heinkel He 100 V-6 experimental fighter (WNr 3002) which belonged to the batch bought from Germany in 1940 photographed at NII VVS. Note that the aircraft is devoid of any markings.

world record at 746.604 km/h flown by Hans Dieterle on 30 March 1939) was demonstrated to the Soviet delegation touring the German aviation factories on 30 October 1939 at Marienehe. The Soviet NII VVS pilot Stepan P. Suprun flew the He 100 during the visit "after only 10 minutes of instructions", and according to Ernst Heinkel astonished the German hosts (including the Heinkel factory test-pilots) by performing advanced aerobatics for half an hour. According to Gen I.F. Petrov (Director of TsAGI) the Germans were not willing to let Suprun try the He 100 as he had not attended the required three months technical type introduction course. Only after Petrov had explained that Suprun was an experienced test pilot and had already studied the aircraft theoretically, was permission to let him fly the He 100 granted by *Reichsmarschall* Hermann Göring over the telephone. Petrov was however forced to sign an obligation that the USSR would pay compensation if the aircraft was destroyed, and also a second document stating that in case of a fatal accident the Heinkel company would not be held responsible for the death of the Soviet test-pilot. Without telling Suprun (in order not to distress him) Petrov calmly signed the documents required. (Suprun was made a Hero of the Soviet Union on 20 May 1940, and for the second time posthumously on 22 July 1941, after being killed in action on 4 July 1941 as CO of the voluntary 401 IAP consisting of NII VVS test-pilots).

Six He 100s (ie the He 100 V1, V2, V4, V5, V6 and V7) were delivered from Germany to the Soviet Union in 1940. At NII VVS Suprun was to continue the testing with Pyotr S. Onopriyenko as test-engineer. Among the test-pilots flying the He 100 at NII VVS was also Grigori Ya. Bakhchivandzhi (1908-1943), who is best known for the testing of the first Soviet rocket-powered interceptor BI-1 designed by Aleksandr Ya. Bereznyak (1912-74) and Aleksei M. Isayev (1908-71). Bakhchivandzhi, who had carried out the first flight of the experimental BI-1 on 15 May 1942, was killed during the seventh test flight on 27 March 1943, and posthumously made a Hero of the Soviet Union 30 years later, on 28 April 1973. (For picture of BI-1, *see* page 37.)

Pyotr M. Popelnyeshenko was the leading test-pilot of the He 100 at LII, where it was also flown by Aleksei I. Grinchik and others. According to the NII VVS engineer Rabkin, only three He 100s were acquired by the Soviet Union, but these three could well be the aircraft allocated to NII VVS, the other three going to LII which was a separate entity.

The Soviet specialists were particularly fascinated by the surface-evaporation cooling system of the He 100, generating a very distinct sound, with steam clouds emerging from the wings after landing.

The Soviet specialists quickly noted however the deficiencies of the He 100: limited longitudinal stability, high wind-loading (resulting in high landing speed: 159 km/h at 2,444 kg landing weight), weak armaments (only two machine-guns) etc.

One of the He 100s was subsequently displayed at the comparative exhibition at TsAGI.

Note: For "He 113" see the section on Focke-Wulf Fw 190.

Heinkel He 111

According to the memoirs of P.M. Stefanovskiy (head of the Flight Testing Department of NII VVS) and A.D. Yakimenko (CO 13 Guards IAD, ex-294 IAD) at least one Heinkel He 111 medium bomber was delivered to NII VVS in early 1941. However, V.B. Shavrov does not list the He 111 among the aircraft purchased from Germany in his monumental *History of the Soviet Aircraft Design.*

The aircraft referred to by Stefanovskiy and Yakimenko is probably the He 111B-1 25 • 32, which landed intact on the Republican side on 17 December 1937 during the Spanish Civil War (*see* Chapter 1 for details). This aircraft was already dispatched to the Soviet Union for investigations in February 1938, which Stefanovskiy and Yakimenko presumably did not know when they saw it at NII VVS in 1941.

A number of He 111s were however captured and test-flown, and even used operationally by the Red Air Force during the war.

After the Stalingrad battle the retreating German forces left about 20 serviceable He 111, Ju 87 and Bf 109 aircraft (their empty fuel tanks indicating the German supply problems at Stalingrad) at their former base at Bolshaya Rossoshka between Volga and Don. The Military Gliding School of the Parachute Forces (*Saratovskaya Voyenno-aviatsionnaya planernaya shkola vozdushno-desantnykh vojsk*; SVAPSh VDV) at Saratov was invited to choose captured aircraft of their liking to replenish their diminishing park of glider-towing aircraft. Five pilots from SVASh were ferried from Saratov in an obsolete Tupolev TB-3 heavy bomber. Upon arrival they were greeted by the Soviet "war booty collecting task force":

'Right boys, please choose yourselves a "Fritz" or a "Hans"!'

No one of the SVAPSh group had any experience of German aircraft or understood the German language. The pilots however bravely entered the cockpits and tried to identify the instruments, levers and knobs, marking them with a piece of chalk. Grigori A. Usov, like the other pilots with two-engine experience on the Tupolev SB-2s, selected an He 111, started the engines, taxied along the runway, crossed himself and took off. He was soon joined in the air by the other pilots ferrying He 111s — still in German markings (!) to Saratov. At Saratov a trigger-happy anti-aircraft battery opened fire and hit the wing of Sen-Lt Petrakov's aircraft. He was however able to land successfully. Another batch of He 111s was ferried from Gumrak, together with a German POW pilot and an interpreter. The German pilot was questioned about the He 111's equipment and handling characteristics. When he realized that the Soviet pilots did not use parachutes he refused to enter the aircraft, but was later given a Soviet parachute (the Soviets obviously did not bother about such details for themselves!) and participated in a number of instructional flights. At Saratov a "train" of two, later even three cargo gliders were towed by each He 111. Night flying training was also immediately started with He 111s.

Of the pilots flying He 111s at Saratov the following are mentioned by name: the CO of the Latvian escadrille Aleksandrs Auguls, Krasnoyurchenko, Voronkov, Kruglov, Voroshilov, Petrosyan and Larin.

An He 111 was also used for towing Antonov A-7 transport gliders supporting partisans in the Baltic area in 1943.

One black-painted He 111 without any national insignia, obviously used by the Soviets for clandestine operations, was shot down over the Gulf of Finland on

A Heinkel He 111H-11 bomber powered by two Jumo 210 F-1 engines being tested at NII VVS. On the original print the red star on the fuselage is clearly visible, and a Douglas C-47 can also be identified in the background.

20 October 1942 by the top-scoring Finnish fighter ace Flight-Master Ilmari Juutilainen of 3./LeLv 24 with his Brewster BW-364. That the Finnish Air Force was aware of the fact that the Soviets used captured German aircraft for clandestine missions — such as dropping of partisans and *desants* behind the lines, and subsequently did not take any risks, is proven by the fact that another Finnish Brewster-ace, Capt. Veikko Karu of LeLv 26 intercepted and shot down another Heinkel He 111 over the Karelian Isthmus on 25 May 1943. Unfortunately this time a German clandestine operation *"Unternehmen Karl"* to drop a reconnaissance and sabotage group including volunteer Russian ex-POWs near the Arkhangelsk railway was in question, and because of a mistake the *Abwehr* had not informed the co-belligerent Finnish Air Force of the flight of the He 111 which was to cross the Finnish lines. As a result the officer in charge of the mission, *Sonderführer* Schwarze and three of the participants were killed.

A detailed photograph of the bomb load of a Heinkel He 111 at NII VVS. Note the pointed red star on the fuselage, and the Ilyushin Il-2 *Shturmovik* in the rear.

The fuselage of a Heinkel He 111 (1T + KX of the little-known KG 28) is transported through Moscow in late autumn 1941.

This Heinkel He 111 (1H + AK, WNr 3773) of KG 26 which was captured on 17 December 1941 at Kalinin seems to be in repairable condition.

Maj-Gen Georgi N. Zakharov (CO 303 IAD) tested an He 111 in 1943. This bomber had made a forced landing after a reconnaissance flight over the Soviet rear areas when it was hit by AA fire. The German pilot tried to find a suitable field to land, and did not notice that the landing site chosen was in fact a camouflaged Soviet fighter base! The He 111 pilot turned out to be a specialist on the Luftwaffe radio-communication system, and gave away much valuable information during questioning, enabling the Soviets to listen-in to various Luftwaffe networks and frequencies. Col. Yevgeni V. Koyander (Deputy Signals Commander of the 1st Air Army) regrets however that the information received was not duly put to good use, as the listening service of the Red Air Force was organized on an "acceptable level" only in 1944.

Two He 111s were received at NII VVS for testing on 25 March 1943: one H-6 and one H-11 subtype. The first one (H-6) was damaged during the test flights, but the second (H-11) was fully tested by Col G. Ashitkov in May 1943. At NII VVS the speed, ceiling and range were considered unsufficient regardless of the supercharged Jumo Ju 211F-1 engines (the He 111 was primarily compared to the Il-4 long-distance bomber, standard equipment of ADD). This aircraft was subsequently displayed at the war booty exhibition in Moscow in June 1943.

In summer 1944 the pilot Nikolai G. Kovtykh of 23 OAP GVF (in the 1970s Deputy Minister of Civil Aviation) discovered an intact-looking He 111 with "fascist" insignia on the ground in the newly-recaptured Ukraine from his Polikarpov Po-2 light liaison aircraft. Kovtykh landed beside the German aircraft in order to investigate what had happened, and found out that the passengers onboard consisted of the Central Committee of the underground Slovakian Communist Party, trying to deliver an urgent message to Moscow and to have a meeting with Stalin! He assisted the Heinkel to fly to his regiment's main base, from where the delegation was subsequently forwarded to Moscow. Afterwards it was found out that the persons involved were preparing an uprising in Slovakia. (This aircraft was obviously He 111 H-10 WNr 5313, coded "S-82" of the Slovakian AF. The aircraft was piloted by Capt Ludovit Koza, who on 2 August 1944 headed east from Tri Duby, Slovakia.)

A Heinkel He 111 (WNr 701678) captured by the Soviet forces at Posen (now Poznan, Poland) on 7 February 1945. A total of 292 German aircraft and a great number of transport gliders were captured in the Posen area.

A highly spectacular POW escape took place from the Usedom Island (where the Peenemünde missile test centre was located) in the Baltic Sea on 8 February 1945 when Sen-Lt Mikhail P. Devyatayev took off in an He 111 bomber, carrying another nine Soviet POWs as passengers. Devyatayev landed the IIe 111 after a two-hour flight at Woldenberg, 8 km behind the front lines, where the He 111 crew and passengers were picked up by soldiers from the 38th Artillery Regiment of the 61st Army, 2nd Belorussian Front. Devyatayev, who belonged to the 104 Guards IAP (ex-298 IAP, which was made a Guards unit on 25 August 1943), had been shot down in an Airacobra over the Lvov-Brody area on his 180th mission on 13 July, 1944, having scored a total of 9 victories. He was only made a Hero of the Soviet Union 12 years after the war, on 15 August 1957. The delay can only indicate that Devyatayev was suspected of being a German agent.

Heinkel He 162
A number of serviceable Heinkel He 162 jet fighters and other German aircraft were found in the Vienna area by the 212 Guards IAP (ex-438 IAP) in spring 1945. This ex-Luftwaffe base was later handed over to the US Forces, as it was located in the allocated American occupation sector.

A Heinkel He 162 Volksjäger "02" being tested at the *Letno-issledovatelskiy institut* (Flight Test Institute). Note the LII emblem on the tail.

Both NII VVS and LII flight-tested the He 162. On 11 July 1946 the He 162 and the indigenous Yak-15 and MiG-9 jet fighters were demonstrated to the Minister of Aircraft Production Mikhail V. Khrunishev;[18] Deputy Minister Pyotr V. Dementyev,

[18] 1901-61, Minister of Aircraft Production from 1946 to 1953, having been Deputy People's Commissar of Aircraft Production from 1939 to 1942. Later he served for some time as Deputy Chairman of the USSR Council of Ministers, ie Deputy Prime Minister.

the designers Aleksandr S. Yakovlev (who had resigned from the position as Deputy Minister only two days earlier!) and Artyom I. Mikoyan. The Heinkel He 162 was piloted by the LII pilot Georgi M. Shiyanov (HSU 1.5.1957), the Yak-15 by Mikhail I. Ivanov (HSU 5.3.1948, killed "on duty" ie. during a test-flight on 14 July 1948) and the MiG-9 by Aleksei N. Grinchik of LII, who crashed and was killed during his demonstration. This accident considerably delayed the development of Soviet jet aircraft. No comments of the performance of the He 162 compared to that of the Soviet jet fighters are given in Soviet publications.

Note: In contrast to the Messerschmitt Me 262 no air combat against the Heinkel He 162 is reported by Soviet authors.

Henschel Hs 126

At the end of July 1941 Maj A.V. Koronets (CO of 71 IAP of VVS KBF, the Air Force of the Baltic Fleet) sent the engineer of his regiment V.N. Yurchenko to inspect a number of Henschel Hs 126 reconnaissance aircraft of the former Estonian Air Force stored at Jägala. The intention of Maj. Koronets was to find a suitable aircraft for operations in the German rear. The best of three available Hs 126s was chosen, and prepared for use in three days. Maj. Koronets himself flew the aircraft to Ülemiste (in the vicinity of Tallinn) and, starting on the next day, he made a number of reconnaissance flights without any trouble. This Hs 126 was obviously destroyed when the Soviet forces retreated from Tallinn on 27 August 1941. (Col. A.V. Koronets was shot down and killed at Suursaari/ Hogland/ in the Gulf of Finland in combat with Finnish Brewsters of Lentolaivue 24 on 28 March 1942. He was probably the victim of Flight-Master Ilmari Juutilainen of 3./LeLv 24 and his Brewster BW-364, who scored two kills on that day. The 71 IAP was to become 10 Guards IAP on 31 May 1943.)

The Estonian Air Force had acquired at least five Henschel Hs 126Bs in the autumn of 1939. After the Soviet occupation of Estonia in June 1940, what was left of the former Estonian army was reorganized as the 22nd Territorial Corps of the Red Army, with the remnants of the Estonian Air Force reformed into the Aircraft Squadron of the 22nd Corps, with Jägala as its main base. After the German attack on the Soviet Union beginning on 22 June 1941, the 22nd Squadron was ordered to retreat to Russia on 27 June with its few serviceable aircraft (the most potent being a handful of Ansons and Hs 126s). A number of aircraft are reported to have been flown to Russia; all others were burned and destroyed. The Estonian unit of the VVS had thus virtually ceased to exist. (For details of the national Estonian units of the VVS and Luftwaffe, *see* Appendix 2.1.)

Despite the above, the Soviet Baltic fleet apparently found three Henschels that had escaped destruction, from which the aircraft flown by Maj. Koronets was chosen.

Junkers Ju 52/3m

The trimotor Junkers Ju 52/3m was already used at LII for towing big transport

A Junkers W 34 light transport aircraft in Soviet colours in 1945. This obsolete aircraft could only have been used for secondary transport tasks in the rear.

gliders in 1941. It had been tested before that at NII VVS by Pyotr M. Stefanovskiy, who noted that it was equipped with three excellent BMW Hornet engines. A total of 93 flights were made at NII VVS with this aircraft. (The origin of this Ju 52/3m is unclear — it could have belonged to the pre-war Estonian airline company AGO.)

At LII the Ju 52/3m was flown by Aleksei I. Grinchik and Nikolai V. Gavrilov, who evolved methods of towing *"Sokol"* and *"Orel"* transport gliders piloted by Igor I. Shelest and the Tsybin KTs-20 glider piloted by Viktor L. Rastorguyev.

In 1942 a Junkers Ju 52/3m was modified into a "flying laboratory" for TsAGI by the designer Vasili V. Nikitin.[19] After the Battle of Stalingrad approximately 80 captured Ju 52/3m transports were repaired at the GVF repair shops in early 1943 under the supervision of the NII GVF (Civil Aviation Research Institute), providing the necessary technical documentation etc. (As a large number of non-serviceable and non-repairable German transports were found at Gumrak, they were even taken into use as temporary winter quarters for the Soviet soldiers by installing primitive ovens in the aircraft fuselage!)

One of the plants repairing the Junkers transports was the GVF Repair Factory No 243 in Tashkent, Uzbekistan, concentrating on the overhaul of the nine-cylinder BMW radial engines of the Stalingrad war booty. It was fortunate that Soviet-made piston rings were applicable, as original spares were naturally unavailable. (The BMW VI V-12 watercooled engine had been licence-produced in the Soviet Union as M-17 from the end of the 1920s, so there was still a certain commonality between Soviet and German parts). The sturdy Ju 52/3m was extensively used for transport tasks in the Soviet rear, and operated ie. the route Perm-Kuybyshev in the summer of 1944.

[19] Nikitin, 1901-1955, led his own fighter-design bureau OKB-30 from 1938-40, and later worked ie. at TsAGI, ending his professional career designing helicopters at the Kamov OKB.

A pre-war Junkers Ju 52/3m of the German-Soviet joint venture airline Deruluft (note the insignia in Cyrillic print!) at Kaunas, Lithuania.

The Junkers Ju 52/3m was also used on floats in the Soviet Union. Note a Catalina flying-boat in the rear — the photograph seems to have been taken from another Catalina.

The Junkers Ju 52/3m also carried civil registrations in the Soviet Union. The photograph depicts loading of CCCP — L64 at Alikhabad, Azerbaidzhanskaya SSR, 1947.

A Ju 52/3m landed inadvertently at Jaskorajeny, Hungary, held by the 9 Corps PVO on 6 January 1945. The crew (three German officers and two Hungarian sergeants) were taken prisoner.

On 26 February 1945 the advancing Red Army captured the Luftwaffe base at Neukirch (only 3.5 km from Breslau-West, which was still held by German forces). Col-Gen Semyon A. Krasovskiy (CO 2nd Air Army) noticed that the surroundings of Neukirch and Breslau-West were rather similar, and decided to use this similarity to the disadvantage of the surrounded Germans at Breslau.

All Soviet activity at Neukirch was carefully disguised, and the appearance of the base was covertly transformed to look like that of Breslau-West. A nocturnal Polikarpov Po-2 explored the light signals used by the Germans, and the stage was set for a dramatic deception play. A total of 149 tonnes (!) of goods intended for the surrounded German forces were dropped at Neukirch during March-April 1945. A total of five Ju 52/3ms and four transport gliders were duped to land at Neukirch, and even an ex-Soviet Po-2 used by the German commandant of Breslau landed at the Soviet-held Neukirch!

Finally, a Ju 52/3m JU + BM, WNr 500146 was flown from Bromma, Sweden to the Soviet Union via Turku, Finland, on 27 August 1945. This aircraft which belonged to IV./TG 1 had arrived at Bulltofta from Liepaya (Libau), Latvia on 8 May 1945.

The Junkers Ju 352 was used for flight-testing of various engines (the three-engine configuration providing an ideal test bed!). The centre engine (with four-bladed propeller) is presumably a 3000 hp Jumo 222 W-type engine, while the outer engines are probably the ordinary 1000 hp Bramo 323 (the Jumo 222 had already been tested in a Ju 252 at Dessau in summer 1944 with standard 1340 hp Jumo 211s as outer engines). No details about the Soviet use of the Ju 352 test-bed are known (but refer to the Postscript — especially the section on the Junkers OKB in the Soviet Union).

Junkers Ju 87

According to the history of TsAGI a Junkers Ju 87 Stuka dive-bomber was also included in the batch of aircraft delivered from Germany in 1940. Shavrov does not mention this aircraft, however.

As is related in the He 111 section, about 20 serviceable He 111, Ju 87 and Bf 109 aircraft were found by advancing Soviet forces at the former Luftwaffe base at Bolshaya Rossoshka after the Stalingrad battle. Lt Titov of the Military Gliding School of the Parachute Forces *(Saratovskaya Voyenno-aviatsionnaya planernaya shkola vozdushno-desantnykh vojsk;* SVAPSh VDV) at Saratov was given the task of ferrying a Ju 87 to Saratov, but lost his orientation after some problems with the radio-compass, and found himself over the German-held Rostov-on-Don. The Germans however did not pay any attention to the Stuka, so he managed to escape, and landed with zero fuel on the Soviet-held shore of the Don river, where he refilled his fuel tanks again and could continue to Saratov. In Saratov the Ju 87 joined the other foreign aircraft (including a number of Hurricane IIs) at SVAPSh VDV and was piloted among others by Aleksandrs Auguls.

Soviet personnel
inspecting dismantled
Ju 87 Stukas.

An ex-Romanian Junkers
Ju 87 Stuka and a
Messerschmitt Bf 109 are
inspected by Soviet
personnel at an airforce
base in the Crimea,
summer 1944.

A Ju 87D-1 captured at Stalingrad was tested at NII VVS in 1943. The max. bomb load of 1,500 kg, which in the hands of experienced pilots could be dropped very exactly, exceeded the normal payload of the Pe-2 dive bomber almost twice, although the Ju 87D was much slower. A max. speed of 382 km/h at medium altitude and with a bomb-load of 500 kg was recorded. However the low speed of the Stuka made it a rather easy prey for the fast Soviet fighters.

The anti-tank Ju 87 with the 37 mm Oerlikon cannon was also tested at NII VVS. The heavy cannon however impaired considerably the manoeuvrability and speed of this model (speed reduction 50-60 km/h). This aircraft had been captured in spring 1943 at Bryansk together with the pilot Hans Trenkman, who told that 25 Stukas equipped with the 37 mm anti-tank cannon had been dispatched to the Eastern front in February 1943. According to a recent Russian account, Trenkman was an experienced test-pilot who had tested Bf 109s, Ju 88s and Fw 190s at Rechlin, the reason why NII VVS specialists A. Rozanov and A. Aronov participated in the follow-up questioning of Trenkman.

A Stuka was exhibited in Moscow in summer 1943. The origin and identity of this (these?) aircraft has however not been positively established — are the NII VVS or the Saratov-aircraft in question?

A Junkers Ju 87 Stuka (WNr 2754) at NII VVS. The red stars are clearly visible on the original print.

Junkers Ju 88

Two Junkers Ju 88 bombers were delivered from Germany to the Soviet Union in 1940. One of the aircraft was the WL + 008 (possibly WNr 5023), a pre-production Ju 88A-0, which was tested at NII VVS and LII (where it was piloted by Igor I. Shelest and others). At LII it was demonstrated to a group of designers from Tupolev's OKB, headed by the Deputy Chief Designer Aleksandr A. Arkhangelskiy.

At NII VVS it was immediately noted that the main task of the JU 88 was dive-bombing (ability to attach big bombs under the wings, with bomb-dropping envelope clearing the propellers, air-brakes under wings, automatic diving and take-up control systems, excellent pilot vision, etc). With a flight weight of 10,350 kg, a max. speed of 365 km/h at ground level and 445 km/h at 5,600 m was established. Climbing time to 5000 m was 18 minutes.

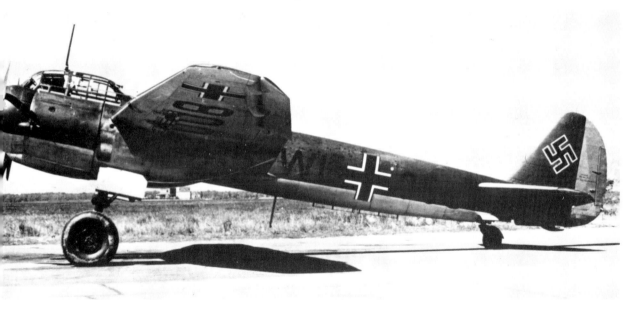

One of the two Junkers Ju 88A-0s bought from Germany in 1940 was the WL + 008, which was tested by Igor I. Shelest at LII.

As already mentioned in the section on the Dornier Do 215, the NII VVS test pilots Valentin I. Khomyakov and Fyodor F. Opadchiy were ordered to organise a special reconnaissance unit after the German attack on 22 June 1941. This unit was to consist of a number of Spanish pilots who had arrived in the Soviet Union after the Spanish Civil War, and was to be equipped with the German aircraft which had already been tested at NII VVS (ie the Dornier Do 215, Junkers Ju 88, Messerschmitt Bf 110 and Bf 109 — three of each). At the end of the training period in the Urals region, Opadchiy was badly injured in an accident with a Ju 88. The aircraft, piloted by the Spaniard Manuel Leon, with Opadchiy as co-pilot and Jose Ignatio Aginaga as flight-engineer, crashed on take-off. Opadchiy suffered serious burns rescuing Leon who broke one leg in the crash, while Aginaga had only minor wounds. Opadchiy was hospitalized for over 18 months, but after great efforts he was able to return to test-flying, becoming Chief test-pilot of the Myasishchev KB in 1943, and later working at the Tupolev OKB (testing the Tu-4, Tu-16 and other aircraft, for which he was made an HSU on 7 February 1957).

On 25 June 1941 a Ju 88 (B3 + BM, WNr 2428) of 4./KG 54 landed near Kiev, the German crew having deserted. Upon questioning by Soviet security forces the crew, consisting of *Uffz* Hans Herrmann, navigator *Uffz* Hans Kratz, *O Gefr* Adolf Appel and radio-operator *Uffz* Wilhelm Schmid, declared that they did not want to fight against the Soviet people. They had dropped their bombs in the Dnepr. On the same day they wrote an appeal to their fellow "German pilots and soldiers" which read; "Brother pilots and soldiers — follow our example. Kill Hitler and come here to Russia." Their appeal was widely spread by the Soviet forces and was also published in *Pravda* of 29 June 1941. After two days another appeal of a crew member of 1./KG 54, flight mechanic Gefr Paul Hofbauer was published: "Brothers against Hitler and fascism! Come over to Soviet Russia!" His aircraft, B3 + BH (WNr 7158) piloted by *Fw* Karl Fiege had already been shot down and made a forced-landing on 24 June 1941 at Ovruch.

On 8 July 1941 at 0400 in the morning, three Ju 88s landed near Lake Peipus (or Chudskogo Ozero) which separates Estonia from main Russia, and the crews are said to have made no resistance.

It is not known in what condition these aircraft had force-landed and were taken over by the Russians, but they were certainly thoroughly inspected.

The Junkers Ju 88 (4D + —) of KG 30 in the picture was probably the first aircraft shot down by the VVS SF in the Great Fatherland War. It seems to have made a rather successful crash-landing after being forced down by Capt Boris Safonov of the 72 AP on 24 June 1941 at Zelentsa in the Murmansk area. The Ju 88 crew consisting of Jacob Mercinetz, Hans Hartmann and Josef Markwort were taken prisoners.

Lt-Col V.F. Golubev, CO of the 4 Guards IAP of VVS KBF inspecting a force-landed Junkers Ju 88G (?), WNr 620308 in the Baltic area, autumn 1944.

On 7 August 1941 a Ju 88 was displayed at a war booty exhibition in the Kirov District Council Park in Leningrad.

In August 1941 a force-landed Ju 88 was brought to the 42 IAP (to become 133 Guards IAP on 8 October 1943) commanded by Maj. Fyodor I. Shinkarenko (HSU 7.4.1940 after the Soviet-Finnish Winter War), who also planned to use it for reconnaissance flights over the German rear in the Orel area. The aircraft was repaired by the regiment's engineer I. Dobrin, but he was forced to destroy the Ju 88 to avoid its recapture by the advancing German forces, when the regiment was ordered to retreat to Optukha (near Mtensk).

In autumn 1941 a Ju 88 landed in error at the base of the 38 ORAE on the Western Front (central Russia). The aircraft had taken off from Smolensk for a photo-reconnaissance flight to Yaroslavl, but lost its orientation because of a defective radio-compass, and as fuel was running low the pilot decided to land at the first German-held airfield. When he became aware of his fatal mistake it was already too late. The Soviet personnel eagerly studied the systems and equipment of the German aircraft, and Col. Ye. V. Koyander (the future Deputy Signals Commander of 1st Air Army, who happened to visit the Soviet AF base in question) wanted to dismantle the radio navigation equipment but was instructed to see that the aircraft was ferried to NII VVS for further investigations in intact condition.

On 16 February 1943 a pilot of the Air Force of the Northern Fleet (VVS SF) was killed in a Ju 88 which exploded on take-off in the Murmansk area. The aircraft had made a forced landing and had been repaired by the Soviet engineers.

The Moscow war booty exhibition in 1943 also included a Junkers Ju 88.

A Mistel S1 consisting of a Junkers Ju 88A-4 and a Messerschmitt Bf 109F captured in East Germany in spring 1945 (?) is inspected by Soviet personnel.

Messerschmitt Bf 108 Taifun

Two Messerschmitt Bf 108 Taifun light communications/touring aircraft were delivered from Germany in 1940 (flown among others by Aleksei I. Grinchik of LII). One Taifun was used as a courier aircraft by Pyotr N. Stefanovskiy of NII VVS in 1942 when he was dispatched to the aircraft factory at Omsk in Siberia to test the S-110 fighter prototype designed by Dmitriy L. Tomashevich. (The S-110 had been designed at the NKVD-controlled OKB-29 "*sharaga*" or "engineers' prison" in Moscow where Tomashevich had been interned during the Stalin purges in 1937-38 together with Andrej N. Tupolev, Vladimir V. Myasishshev and Vladimir M. Petlyakov, who all led their own sub-bureaux at OKB-29.)

Messerschmitt Bf 109

This German fighter which was to become the main opponent of the Soviet Air Force was continually of major interest to the Soviet pilots and designers.

A Messerschmitt Bf 109B-1 (coded 6 • 15, flown by *Feldwebel* Otto Polenz) was already captured on 4 December 1937 during the Spanish Civil War, and after testing by a French commission in Spain was quickly transported to the Soviet Union in February 1938 for testing at NII VVS (*see* Chapter 1). It was delivered by train, and assembled by the experienced technical staff led by Ivan V. Zhulev. The Jumo-engined fighter equipped with a fixed-pitch propeller was flown by Stepan P. Suprun, Pyotr N. Stefanovskiy and others. When Suprun was demonstrating aerobatics to the designer N.N. Polikarpov and his engineers the stabilizer bracing fractured, and he was forced to use all his skill to land the aircraft successfully. Suprun was criticized by his superior Stefanovskiy for risking his life instead of parachuting to safety, but he defended himself saying that he was happy to have detected the weak point of the German fighter. Now the reason why "the fascists were known to avoid dog-fights with the sharp-turning I-15s and I-16s in Spain" was revealed, and it was clear why the Germans preferred to perform low-level horizontal attacks.

A Messerschmitt Bf 109B captured in Spain and subsequently transported to the Soviet Union for testing at NII VVS.

In October 1939 Suprun had an opportunity of inspecting the newer "*Emil*" modification at the Messerschmitt factory in Augsburg. Two German officers noticed his special interest in the modified tail-plane construction of the "*Emil*" and asked him on which front he had fought in Spain. The Germans of course did not believe his negative answer. In May 1940 five Bf 109Es purchased in Germany were delivered in crates by train to Moscow (the WNr of one aircraft is known to have been 2738). The young graduate of the *Voyenno-vozdushnaya inzhenernaya akademiya imeni professora N.Ye. Zhukovskogo* (Zhukovskiy Aviation Engineering Academy) Izrail G. Rabkin (who had worked for only one week at NII VVS) was ordered to assemble the German fighters at the Moscow Central Airport, assisted by the experienced engineer Ivan V. Zhulev. The first aircraft was assembled by the two engineers virtually on their own by carefully studying the German technical documentation. Rabkin even ran the engine before a "diplomatical" intermezzo occurred: a black ZIS-101 limousine with three grim-looking passengers arrived, and a representative of the People's Commissariat for Foreign Trade approached the military engineers asking them why the aircraft had been assembled without the presence of the Messerschmitt representative, who had already waited ten days in Moscow for an invitation to take part in the unpacking of the crates! Rabkin answered that the Bf 109 was assembled on orders from his military superiors and that he took no orders from anybody else. Furthermore, in NII VVS nothing was known about the presence of any Messerschmitt engineer! The foreign trade official returned to the car to explain the situation to the Germans, and Rabkin overheard heated comments about an "international conflict" etc, after which the three gentlemen approached him together. The German engineer declared solemnly that on behalf of the Messerschmitt company he protested against the self-indulgent assembly of one of the aircraft sold to the Soviet Union, and that he would not accept any guarantee claims whatsoever concerning this aircraft. Regarding the other "*Emils*" the Messerschmitt company would fulfil its contractual obligations. Rabkin answered drily: "We did not expect any assistance from Germany." Rabkin subsequently rang up his superior Aleksandr S. Voyevodin (Head of the fighter testing department of NII VSS) for advice, and was told to assemble the other aircraft together with the German engineer. He was then present every day, and required Rabkin and Zhulev to sign a document releasing the company from any liability regarding each crate opened, watching that every step was performed according to the instructions.

The German engineer was extremely punctual, Rabkin recalls, and did not miss any opportunity to point this out. Once an ignition coil was found to be defective. The German engineer immediately confirmed that his Company accepted the claim, and that a new coil would arrive at exactly 12.45 hours the day after tomorrow. The new coil was delivered by plane from Berlin two days later, the plane landing at 12.30! The German engineer did not take any notice of the first "109" (assembled in his absence by Rabkin and Zhulev), but worked very meticulously on the other four aircraft. When the first aircraft was ready for flying, Rabkin called Voyevodin. After some time the test-pilot Maj. Aleksandr S. Nikolayev arrived in a Polikarpov U-2 biplane. Rabkin tried to tell him about the characteristics of the Bf 109, but Nikolayev was only interested in the climbing speed of the Bf 109, and did not listen to Rabkin's carefully prepared lecture. Zhulev reassured the disappointed Rabkin telling him that Nikolayev had already flown several German aircraft. After some days another three aircraft were flown away: one to NII VVS and two to LII. The last of the five Bf 109E aircraft was inspected by Stepan P. Suprun, who confirmed it to be the aircraft he had seen in Germany, which thus had been delivered as agreed. This particular aircraft was ferried to NII VVS by Nikolayev, with Stefanovskiy and Suprun, who had arrived in a Fieseler Fi 156 Storch, taking Zhulev and Rabkin with them in the now very crowded Storch for the return flight to NII VVS. Upon arrival at NII VVS Rabkin reported the assembly completed to Voyevodin, and was on the spot appointed leading engineer for the testing of the last aircraft. The tests were to start the very next day, and to be completed in two weeks. A proposal of the test programme and a draft of the corresponding Order of the Day of the Institute was to be presented by 12.00 hours on the following day. The volume of the test programme was to be similar to the tests of the Bf 110. The pilot-engineer Aleksei I. Nikashin assisted the newcomer Rabkin to compile the test programme: first, determination of climbing time to 5000 m, then maximum speed at altitudes of 5000, 4000, 3000, 2000 and 1000 metres. And so on. Rabkin now also saw his test group for the first time — for which the deadline given was accepted as natural! Rabkin's first day as the leading test engineer ended only at ten o'clock at night. And so it was to continue.

Rabkin was at work early each morning in order to prepare himself before the others arrived. At least three flights a day had to be performed, and only serious defects permitted deviation from this norm. At night Rabkin tried to compile the written reports based on the flight tests made by Sharapov who was the leading test-pilot in his group. The Bf 109E had considerably more engine power than the Bf 109B (1150 hp against 650 hp), correspondingly generating a speed of 440 km/h at ground level and 546 km/h (at 5000 m altitude) against 470 km/h of the Bf 109B. The speed of the Bf 109E alarmingly exceeded considerably that of the Soviet standard fighters: the I-16 was almost 100 km/h slower, and the I-153 biplane more than 100 km/h slower.

Comparable results of the State tests with the Yak-1 (I-26) and LaGG-3 (I-301) prototypes were already available — the Yak developed a max speed of 592 km/h and LaGG — 605 km/h. The MiG-1 prototype (I-200) was even faster — 628 km/h at 7200 m altitude. The speed advantage of the German fighter in comparison to the Polikarpov duo in service left however no doubt of the urgent need to complete the development of the new fighter generation. As coming events were to show, the time available was not sufficient to have the new Soviet fighters fully developed before the German attack. The armament and various systems were studied carefully, as were also all structural details, especially from the maintenance point of view. The Soviet engineers noticed that standard joints and interfaces were used in all systems: for connection of ground power, in the cockpit etc. This high degree of standardization was obviously something unknown in the Soviet Union.

The Bf 109E climbed to 5000 m in 6.3 minutes, ceiling being 10,000m. The armament was heavier than was used in the Soviet fighters: the German fighter was, in addition to machine-guns, equipped with two underwing 20 mm Oerlikon cannons. The ammunition weight of a one second fire-burst of the Bf 109E was 2.49 kg, or more than double that of any contemporary fighter, including that of the I-200 prototype.

In order to avoid any subjective appraisal the aircraft was flown by a total of seven test-pilots, including the Director of the NII VVS Maj. Gen Aleksandr I. Filin, his Deputy A.I. Kabanov, A.N. Zhuravchenko and Grigoriy Ya. Bakhchivandzhi. After some days the final report was compiled. Filin required the leading test-engineers to personally present the report — which would be Rabkin's third meeting with the Director. Their first meeting took place during the low-altitude speed test (1 km at 50-70 m altitude), the second meeting when Filin flew the Bf 109 himself.

Filin acquainted himself extremely carefully with the aircraft for 40 minutes, requiring very accurate answers. A multitude of guests visited the NII VVS to see the German aircraft: test-pilots, designers and Air Force officers. The full report was presented by Filin and Rabkin in July 1940 at a conference organized by the People's Commissariat for Aircraft Industry and chaired by A.I. Shakhurin assisted by his Deputy A.S. Yakovlev, the participants including all Chief Designers of aircraft, engines and armament. Meanwhile the "Emil" had also been tested at LII. The LII test-pilot Igor I. Shelest has described the appearance of the German aircraft in LII in his memoirs:

"One day in spring 1940 Ivan F. Kozlov (head of the Flight Department of LII) entered the flight room:

Soon German aircraft will arrive here!

"From where? Why to us?"

Kozlov stopped all discussions:

"Don't ask too many questions. Perhaps this is the success of our diplomacy. The important thing is that we will fly them. Seleznev — you will start with the Me 109; Mushtayev, you take the Dornier 215."

The LII pilots noticed that the aircraft were matt-black with the German national insignia, crosses and swastikas overpainted. The inverted crankcase of the engine made an even and unusual sound. The LII pilots flying the Bf 109 included Ivan D. Seleznev, Aleksei N. Grinchik (flying mock combat against Shelest in an I-153), Viktor L. Rastorguyev, Mark L. Gallaj and Shelest himself. The Messerschmitt fighter was generally given very high marks by the Soviet test-pilots and considered a "soldier's aircraft" (*samolet-soldat*).

After completing the flight-tests of the five Bf 109Es bought from Germany, at least one aircraft was dismantled for further study at NII VVS. During the evacuation of NII VVS to Sverdlovsk at the Ural area in autumn 1941, the test-pilot T. Chigarev crashed fatally on 11 October 1941 in one of the Bf 109Es.

A large number of Bf 109s were naturally captured during the war, and test-flown both by the front-line units, in some cases even used operationally; and above all dispatched to the rear for more extensive testing and examination.

Some cases described in the literature are summarized below:

On 20 July 1941 a Bf 109 made a forced landing 20-25 km SE Moloskolovitsky. This aircraft, with seven victory marks on the tail, was taken to Leningrad where it was displayed in the Gosnardom park next to a Ju 88 shot down on 23 June 1941

A Messerschmitt Bf 109F which belly-landed on 20 July 1941 20-25 km SE Moloskolovitsky is seen here on display in the Gosnardom park in the Leningrad area, August 1941. According to published information there were seven victory bars on the tail.

in the Leningrad area. (This Ju 88, piloted by Hans Türmeyer belonged to KGr 806, which tried to attack Leningrad from the north, ie. from Finland — who was still formally neutral until 25 June, when the Red Air Force made a massive, unsuccessful attempt to destroy the Finnish and German aircraft based in Finland on the ground. Hit by anti-aircraft fire Türmeyer's aircraft made a forced landing at Dibuny on the Karelian Isthmus just south of the pre-war Finnish-Soviet border.)

The German fighter pilot Eduard Kromm defected with his Bf 109 at the beginning of August 1941, and landed at a Soviet AF base, after being escorted by Soviet fighters. During the interrogation he related that four pilots in his Luftwaffe unit had been executed because of treacherous behaviour.

On 20 August 1941 a German fighter pilot defected with his Bf 109, landing in the Vyazma region.

The first Bf 109F to have been captured in repairable condition was flown by *Hauptmann* Rolf Pingel of JG 51. He made a forced landing in the Moscow area in autumn 1941. After repairs by 47 IAD based at Tushino, Moscow, his aircraft was tested at NII VVS by A. Proshakov and others. The armament specialists at

NII VVS noted especially the new cannon installed in the propeller shaft: a Mauser MG-151, the calibre of which could be either 15 or 20 mm. A. Proshakov established the max. speed of the Bf 109F to be 510 km/h at ground level, 560 km/h at 2750 m, and 556 km/h at 500 m while he climbed to 5000 m in 5.4 minutes. Top ceiling was 8750 m.

A belly-landed Messerschmitt Bf 109. Note the two victory bars and the thin cross behind the Balkenkreuz.

The enhanced performance of the F-version, compared to the well-known "*Emil*" which was far superior to that of all Soviet fighters including the new Yak-1 at all altitudes up to 4000 m, caused the Director of the NII VVS Gen. Fedorov to write an alarming letter to A.S. Yakovlev on 24 December 1941: "Today we have no fighter which equals the Bf 109F!" The Soviet response to this threat would be the development of the LaGG-3 with M-82 radial engine; ie. the La-5, and corresponding development of the Yak-1 into the Yak-7 engine, and also the I-185 project of N. N. Polikarpov (which never reached series production status).

In May 1942 a Bf 109 made a forced landing at Volchansk after the pilot had become disorientated (his home base being Ternovaya). This aircraft was evacuated to the rear, while the pilot was taken for questioning to the 21st Army Headquarters.

Another Bf 109 was flown by Aleksandr I. Pokryshkin[19] at Novocherkassk.

---

[19] The Soviet No 2 fighter ace, who was to score a total of 59 victories; one of two triple pilot-HSUs: 24.4.1943, 24.8.1943 and finally on 19.8.1944.

Pokryshkin has given a number of slightly varying accounts in different editions of his memoirs: "in spring 1942 I was summoned by my CO, V.P. Ivanov, (16 Guards IAP, ex-55 IAP) to the (216) IAD headquarters at Novocherkassk from our base in the Krasnodon area. I was informed by the Division Deputy CO that a Croatian pilot had defected with a Bf 109 (obviously of 15./JG 52). The Bf 109 was to be used by a Special test group headed by Maj. Telegin, which was subordinated to the Deputy CO of the Air Force of the Southern Front Gen. Nikolai F. Naumenko (1901-67, later CO of the 4th and 15th Air Armies etc.). As a member of the special test group Pokryshkin made a number of flights in the Bf 109, frightening the crew of a Tupolev SB-2 bomber and a Polikarpov Po-2 liaison aircraft who did not pay any attention to the fresh red stars on the fuselage of the Messerschmitt and made forced landings. After some days even a reconnaissance flight to the Taganrog area was carried out. A captain of the special task group flew to the front line "to check how a Messerschmitt with red stars is received". He was forced to land after engine failure, and was nearly lynched by the Soviet soldiers thinking that they had found an enemy agent! Gen. Naumenko and Pokryshkin had to visit the trigger-happy unit in order to free the task group pilot. After some time Pokryshkin was given the task of flying mock combat in the Bf 109 on behalf of a film team. On landing one undercarriage leg was broken, and the aircraft was damaged beyond repair.

Pokryshkin's comments of the Bf 109 are interesting:

"The aircraft was equipped with a high-performance radio, had a reinforced windscreen front window and a headlight, the cover of which could be ejected. These were features we had only dreamed about . . . But the Bf 109 also had serious deficiencies: the diving characteristics were worse than those of the MiG-3. This was already known to me from combat experience, when I had to escape from Messerschmitts on a recce flight. The German aircraft recovered slower from a steep dive followed by vertical manoeuvres. These deficiencies I put in my mind and decided to utilize them when planning air combat manoeuvres . . ."

At the end of 1942 Ivan A. Vishnaykov (171 IAP; HSU 23.2.1948) was ordered to study a captured Bf 109. After three familiarisation flights he was ready to ferry the Bf 109F to Yelets. He was escorted by three Mikoyan MiG-3s, but was nevertheless fired on by his own anti-aircraft artillery when landing for refuelling. At this refuelling location he was furthermore arrested as a suspected German agent! Only on the following day was he able to continue to Yelets where he was met by his Regimental CO Orlyakin.

After a few days he was again ordered to ferry another Bf 109F to Yelets. At the 171 IAP mock combat was arranged against a MiG-3 piloted by Konstantin F. Sobolev (HSU 15.5.1946) and an La-5 flown by Aleksandr G. Shevtsov (HSU 8.9.1943); a Yak-1 and a P-39 Airacobra were also flown against the Messerschmitt. The La-5 was especially found to be superior, executing a full 360 degrees turn in 18.5 seconds against the 21 seconds of the Bf 109.

The Soviet No 2 fighter ace, triple-HSU Aleksandr Pokryshkin inspecting a former Luftwaffe base in the winter of 1945: a burning Focke-Wulf Fw 189 and a Bf 109. (Note Pokryshkin's vehicle: a US-made Willys Jeep!)

In the summer of 1942 two Bf 109s were used for mock combat trials by the 434 IAP (to become 32 Guards IAP on 21 November 1942) in the Stalingrad area.

According to an article in *Krasnaya Zvezda* two Bf 109s were forced down at Kotelnikovo by Sergei D. Luganskiy of the 270 IAP (twice HSU, 2.9.1943 and 1.7.1944, scored a total of 37 personal and 6 "group" victories) and I.F. Kuzmichev of the same regiment (later to become 152 Guards IAP). These German aircraft were used for a surprise raid on Taganrog, each aircraft carrying two 50 kg bombs. The attack was performed by Ivan M. Korniyenko and Kuzmichev, who bombed a German car park from low altitude.

However, in his own memoirs Luganskiy gives a different account of this incident, indicating the date of the capture as late autumn 1941. According to Luganskiy the German pilots were forced down by Maj. Fyodor Telegin (CO of 270 IAP) and himself after the Soviet pilots became aware that the Germans had run out of ammunition. After inspection of the German aircraft Maj. Telegin decided to use one of them for clandestine reconnaissance tasks, with the aircraft still carrying German national insignia. After a number of such flights, which obviously did not give any suspicion to the German ground forces used to single German aircraft performing *"freie Jagd"* missions, Maj. Telegin's Bf 109 was finally hit by German AA artillery, but he was able to make a forced landing on Soviet-held territory.

Another defection by a Croatian pilot in a Bf 109 is described by the fighter pilot Vladimir D. Lavrinenkov (HSU 1.5.1943 and 1.7.1944; to score a total of 35 personal and 11 "group" victories) in his memoirs. The Croatian pilot landed at Chuyevo in July 1943, the home base of the 9 Guards IAP (ex-69 IAP, Guards on 7 March 1943). The Bf 109 was subsequently tested by the Regimental CO, Maj. Lev L. Shestakov (HSU 10.2.1942; killed in action on 13.3.1944), Lavrinenkov and others.

A Messerschmitt Bf 109F at Stalingrad in February 1943.

A winter-camouflaged Messerschmitt Bf 109F is being tested at Stalingrad in February 1942. Note the underwing MG 151 20 mm cannon.

A dark-camouflaged Messerschmitt Bf 109F-4 with red stars.

A Messerschmitt Bf 109F at the Moscow front in the winter of 1942. This aircraft is said to have been captured at its base, filled up with fuel, and in perfect condition! Note the eight victory bars.

A Messerschmitt Bf 109F ("White 6") with red stars at NII VVS.

In July 1943 two Bf 109s made forced landings at Chuguyev after the leading aircraft was hit by anti-aircraft artillery which destroyed the radio. The inexperienced wingman blindly followed his leader, and landed as well! Next day the two aircraft were taken to the 5 Guards IAP (one of the very first Guards units, ex-129 IAP which was made Guards on 6 December 1941) where some minor damage was repaired. Soon a test-pilot arrived to ferry the aircraft to the NII VVS.

In July 1943 two Croatian pilots (of 15./JG 52 based at Anapa on the Black Sea) defected, after having tried to cover the defection by simulating air combat, and landed at a Soviet base near Tikhoretskaya. The defected pilots who had taken topographical maps, flight books and other documents with them were taken to the HQ of the 57 Guards IAP (ex-36 IAP, which had been made Guards a few months earlier on 8 February 1943). During questioning the Croatian pilots made it clear that they had encountered Spitfires in the air (57 Guards IAP was one of the few Soviet AF regiments equipped with Spitfire Mk Vb): "the Messerschmitt dives better than the Spitfire, because it is heavier, but the Spitfire climbs better" (compare the comments of Pokryshkin!). At the time of the defection the 57 Guards IAP had already converted to other aircraft, and the Croatian pilots were asked to explain how they knew of the Spitfires. They related that they had encountered Spitfires many times, especially on 8 June 1943 at Temruchka when escorting a Focke-Wulf Fw 189 Uhu. At that time the Croatians had already decided to defect, and were only simulating attacks.

The appearance of the *Gustav*-model and its superiority at the Soviet-German front from August 1942 onwards caused even the Director of NII VVS to appeal directly to Stalin on 23 October 1942, urging him to have the development of new Soviet fighters speeded up. The following performance was considered a minimum: take-off weight max 3,300 kg, max. speed at ground level 550-560 km/h, and at 6,000-7,000 m altitude 680-700 km/h.

After the capitulation of the Germans at Stalingrad an intact *Gustav* was finally captured. Capt. A. Proshakov of NII VVS ferried the aircraft to NII VVS, where it was put through the normal test sequence. The *Gustav* (which in the NII VVS accounts is called the "five-point" Messerschmitt) was equipped with the more powerful DB-605A engine, and two underwing Mauser MG-151 20 mm cannons, with the corresponding one-second burst of 4.78 kg. The pilot was further protected by an armoured shield from the rear. A max. speed of 505 km/h at ground level and 650 km/h at 7,000 m altitude was recorded, while it climbed to 5,000 m in 5.1 minutes with a take-off weight of 3235 kg. Top ceiling was 11,200 m. The tests of the new La-5 showed that the new Soviet fighter had inferior characteristics at altitudes above 3000 m, and was equal or slightly superior to the *Gustav* only at ground level. However the weight of the underwing cannons had a clear negative effect on the performance of the *Gustav,* and was not very popular in the Luftwaffe.

NII VVS soon got another Bf 109G-2 (WNr 14513) for testing — this aircraft lacked the underwing cannons, and was correspondingly called the "three-point"

The Messerschmitt Bf 109G-4/R6 "White 2" (WNr 14997, ex-KJ + GU) of *Uffz* Herbert Meissler, 7./JG 52 was forced down by Capt P.T. Tarasov of the 812 IAP on 28 May 1943. In the picture A.I. Novikov, air gunning assistant to the commander of the 3 IAK reports the successful capture of the enemy fighter to Gen. Yevgeniy Ya. Savitskiy (CO of the 3 IAK) who personally arrived at the base of the 812 IAP to inspect the Bf 109.
Note the 15 victory bars on the tail.

Messerschmitt. This aircraft reached max. speed 16-19 km/h greater than that of the "five-point" *Gustav*. With a take-off weight of 3023 kg it climbed to 5000 m in a record 4.4 minutes. The new Yak-1, Yak-7b and Yak-9 in production since beginning of 1943 and all lend-lease fighters delivered to USSR were considered to be inferior to the Bf-109G-2.

On 28 May 1943 Capt. Pavel T. Tarasov (HSU 13.4.1944; killed in action 29.7.1944) and Ltn. S.P. Kalugin of the 812 IAP forced a Bf 109 to land at their base. This was the aircraft of *Uffz* Herbert Meissler (Bf 109 G-4/R6, WNr 14997, "white 2" of 7./JG 52). The capture of an intact Bf 109G was immediately reported to Gen. Yevgeni Ya. Savitskiy (CO of 3 IAK) who arrived personally at the 812 IAP. After inspection and the necessary light repairs the Bf 109 was flown by Gen. Savitskiy himself in mock combat against the Regimental CO Maj. A.U. Yeremin in a Yak. It was found that the Yak turned and climbed faster than the Messerschmitt. Savitskiy toured all air bases under his command (regiment COs Papkov, Isakov, Doroshenkov and Simonov) and demonstrated the German fighter until the engine broke down, and he had to belly-land — fortunately in the vicinity of an aerodrome. The most important fact established was that the pilots now knew the Messerschmitt could be shot down. The aircraft was later sent to Moscow and displayed at the war booty exhibition. Savitskiy was simultaneously summoned to Stalin, and gave a favourable report concerning the abilities of the Yak fighters in combat with the Messerschmitt. Savitskiy was accompanied to the Kremlin by the Deputy Commander of the VVS Gen. Aleksei V. Nikitin who gave him last minute advice: "If you are asked a question, give a short and clear answer. Plauderers are not liked there . . ."

Note 1: Christopher Shores has published a photo of *Uffz* Meissler's Bf 109 showing the whole nose section of the aircraft covered by black smoke. This picture was obviously taken a few moments later than the photographs published here, and if the aircraft really caught fire during the Soviet attempts to start its engine it is uncertain whether Gen. Savitskiy really carried out his demonstration flights with this very aircraft.

Note 2: A Luftwaffe intelligence report dated 27 September 1943 notes that the 812 IAP had probably as many as nine Bf 109s in operational service.

Among the Soviet aces who tested the Bf 109s were Sultan Amet-khan of 9 Guards IAP (*see* page 47) and Mikhail S. Tvelenev (of the same regiment; HSU 23.2.1945, scoring 28 personal and 18 shared victories).

That the Bf 109 was used for clandestine operations by the Soviet Air Force was witnessed among others by the fighter ace Arseni V. Vorozheikin (twice HSU on 4.2 and 19.8.1944, scoring a total of 52 victories) in his memoirs: "A Bf 109 landed at the base of the 728 IAP at Solntsevo near Kursk. This aircraft was already "ours" and was piloted by Anatoli S. Komosa, Piloting Inspector of the 2nd Air Army." (HSU on 27.6.1945 with 19 personal and 4 "group" victories). Vorozheikin mentions another mysterious Bf 109 used by the Soviets early in the war: his regiment received a message that a 109 would land after performing two rolls over the runway. The aircraft must not be fired upon, and all required assistance was to be given to the pilot without any questions. A pilot dressed in a German uniform flew the 109 and soon after his landing a transport aircraft arrived from Moscow and carried the pilot and his flight bag back to the Soviet capital. "Could this have been a Soviet agent in the Luftwaffe?" — Vorozheikin concludes his account.

When sufficient numbers of Bf 109 became available, mock combat demonstrations were arranged on a regular basis. In January 1943 a main Administration "for Combat Preparation of the Frontal Aviation" was founded at the Headquarters of the VVS, commanded by Gen. D.F. Kondratyev with Col. Sergei I. Mironov (HSU on 7.4.1940 after the Soviet-Finnish Winter War) as his deputy. This body organized a demonstration team consisting of the fighter aces Nikolai I. Khramov (HSU 23.2.1948, total score 16 personal and 4 "group" victories) and M.S. Sapronov flying Bf 109s, and correspondingly Pyotr S. Sereda (HSU

23.11.1942), Aleksandr P. Silantyev (HSU 17.12.1941; later became Aviation Marshal and in 1969 1st Deputy CO of the Soviet Air Force) and Aleksandr F. Semyonov (HSU 21.3.1940 after the Soviet-Finnish Winter War) flying Yak fighters. This team toured reserve fighter regiments and aviation schools in the rear. In order to make the combat demonstrations more realistic they flew the Bf 109s in original German insignia (!) causing even anti-aircraft artillery regiments, warned in advance, to open fire. It was thought that the Soviet pilots would attack more aggressively if they saw the black German crosses! In Kopajgorod Maj. M.S. Sapronov performed mock combat against Georgi N. Prokopenko (CO of the 3 Guards IAP, ex-155 IAP, which was one of the first Guards units from 6 December 1941. Prokopenko received his HSU award on 4 February 1944, and was killed in action on 14 July 1944) whose regiment had only recently converted to the La-5. Prokopenko was judged the winner because of the supreme vertical manoeuvrability of the La-5. All spectators were convinced that the German fighter could be defeated, especially by the new Soviet fighters.

According to another account the performance of the Bf 109G-2 was also the subject of a conference at Lyubertsi, where A. Nikashin of NII VVS flew the Bf 109G-2 in mock-combat against an La-5 with the M-82FN supercharged engine. Only now a Soviet fighter was considered superior to the *Gustav*!

In autumn 1943 NII VVS received a Bf 109G-4 (WNr 19968) for testing. It was tested by A. Proshakov in October 1943. Only slight differences compared to the Bf 109G-2 were noted, among others the fixed rear wheel which had replaced the retractable wheel of the earlier subtype.

In autumn 1943 NII VVS also produced a number of instructional cinema films ("The German fighter Me 109", "Air combat between La-5 and Me 109G-2" etc) which were displayed at various Air Fighting Schools. The CO of the 3rd Air Army wrote to the Director of NII VVS Gen. P. Losyukov: " The movie is needed not only for the fighter units, but also for the aviators of all other regiments. The production of similar movies should be speeded up by all means."

Messerschmitt Bf 109s were also permanently assigned to aviation schools, eg. the *Yejskoye Aviatsionnoye Uchilishche imeni Stalina* (Yejsk Military Aviation School of the Naval Air Force).

In spring 1944 three Bf 109Es were found intact at the former German airfield Veseloye, recaptured by the Soviet forces advancing towards the Crimea. Gen. Yevgeni Ya. Savitskiy decided to personally use one of these for reconnaissance operations over the Crimea. During one of the preparatory flights he was nearly arrested by the Deputy CO of the 52nd Army, Gen. V.N. Razubayev, who was astonished to see Savitskiy in a German aircraft dressed in a black leather jacket without proper insignia of rank!

Gen. Timofey T. Khryukin (CO of the 8th Air Army) was at first unwilling to give Savitskiy permission to carry out the recce missions in a German aircraft, but then requested him to present a detailed flight plan. Savitskiy was to be escorted by four Yakovlev fighters to the city of Sak, from where he would fly alone over the

Black Sea. From the direction of the sea he would fly over the Luftwaffe base at Khersones, and return to the Black Sea via Sevastopol where the escorting Yaks would be waiting.

The next day Gen. Khryukin informed Savitskiy that "permission to execute the plan is granted from above" (who exactly was hidden behind this intriguing phrase is not explained).

The first mission was carried out according to plan, and the recce results transmitted to Gen. Khryukin. As Savitskiy did not receive his next recce tasks as expected he decided — eagerly awaiting the reaction of his superiors — to carry it out the following evening without formal permission.

Savitskiy recorded about 80 German aircraft at Khersones, and the construction of new defence lines at the Sapun hills. On return he was received by his chief of staff Col. Baranov instead of technician Gladkov as expected. Baranov told Savitskiy to immediately report to the furious Gen. Khruykin who was already waiting: "If you fly once more without permission, I will raise the question of your dismissal from the command of 3 IAK". Nevertheless, the energetic Savitskiy was still to fly more such clandestine recce missions with the captured German fighter; the information the courageous pilot brought home flying at an altitude of just 100-150 metres over the German lines was obviously of immense value. The Messerschmitt was later dismantled and dispatched to Moscow together with two other Messerschmitts.

Savitskiy was shot down by German anti-aircraft fire in a Yak fighter on the eve of the major Soviet assault in the Crimea on 11 May 1944. He made a forced landing and was able to escape back to the Soviet lines. On return to his own base he was greeted with congratulations by Col. Baranov: Savitskiy had meanwhile been made a Hero of the Soviet Union and a Lieutenant-General!

Note: the relatively close similarity of the accounts of Croatian pilot-deserters and the clandestine Soviet reconnaissance flight over the Black Sea to Taganrog and the Crimea, and the corresponding relative lack of hard facts makes one suspect that some of the descriptions may be partly intercorrelated "legends". There is no doubt that the Croatians seem to have been rather unreliable allies of the Germans, and with the common Slavic origin they were obviously rather receptive to Soviet propaganda.

Gradually the Soviet Air Force also acquired samples of later Bf 109 modifications:

On 20 September 1944 two Bf 109s were forced to land at Kaunas by pilots of the 125 IAD of the Air Defence Forces (PVO).

On 3 October 1944 a radar-equipped Bf 109G-6 was forced down by Lt Mikhail D. Tsykin of the 31 IAP (HSU 18.8.1945, scoring 15 personal and 6 "group" victories) near Gabrovnitsa (Yugoslavia).

Gen. Georgi N. Zakharov describes in his memoirs how three German pilots deserted with their Bf 109s in East Prussia at the end of 1944. One of these aircraft was tested by Ivan Zamorin.

Gen. Stepan A. Krasovskiy (CO of the 2nd Air Army) describes how a Bf 109 suddenly landed in front of him when inspecting the Heinau transport-glider base occupied by the Soviet Forces in February 1945 (*see* Gotha Go 242 section). The pilot was captured by Krasovskiy's driver Badamshin and the security officer Medvedev. The German pilot had made his very first solo flight and had become disorientated.

As related above, the late model 109s ("*Gustavs*") were tested in the usual manner by experienced test-pilots, including Yuri A. Antipov (who tested both the Bf 109G-4 and the Bf 109G-6), Vladimir Ye. Golofastov and Grigori M. Shiyanov. According to the comments of Shiyanov the Soviet test-pilots gave very high marks to the German fighter, considered an excellent fighter. The simple structure and easy handling characteristics made it suitable for "pilots with relatively low qualifications, coming directly from the pilots schools". In short: a soldier's aircraft (*samolet-soldat*)!

A multitude of BF 109 variants at a former Lutfwaffe base in East Prussia, spring 1945. In the foreground, WNr 412605.

Another ex-JG 3 Messerschmitt Bf 109G-2 (WNr 13903) in January 1943. This aircraft was piloted by *Uffz* Heinrich Blaut (of 3/JG 3) who disappeared on 8 December 1942. As the aircraft seems to be entirely intact it can be presumed that he landed on a Soviet-held airfield. Note the underwing MG 151 20mm cannon.

This Messerschmitt Bf 109G-2 (WNr 14513) of JG 3 has already changed colours in April 1943. Note the JG 3 "Udet" emblem on the nose.

Finally, two Bf 109G-8s were flown to the Soviet Union from Sweden on 27 and 29 August 1945 respectively. These were WNr 230801 and 200049, which had arrived at Bredåkra, Sweden from Kurland, Latvia on 8 May, 1945, the pilots (each aircraft carrying one passenger as well!) trying to escape Soviet occupation and imprisonment.

A Messerschmitt Bf 109K at Praha-Kbely airport in May 1945.

A third Bf 109 (G-10/R3, WNr 130297), with which *Fw* Horst Petzschler of 10./JG 51 had escaped to Bulltofta, Sweden on 4 May 1945, crashed when tested by a Soviet ferry pilot at Bromma on 27 August 1945 before the intended ferry flight to the Soviet Union. The unfortunate Petzschler was handed over to the Soviets by the Swedish authorities in January 1946, remaining a captive in the Soviet Union until September 1949.

A number of encounters with strange Messerschmitt Bf 109s with peculiar insignia (eg. combined *Balkenkreuz* and hammer-and-sickle) were reported by Luftwaffe personnel during the spring of 1945: leaflet dropping on 2 and 3 April 1945 at Königsberg by a Bf 109 with a black-white-red band instead of the *Balkenkreuz* and the inscription FREIES DEUTSCHLAND under the wings. (*See* also the section on the Focke-Wulf Fw 190.)

Messerschmitt Bf 110

Five Messerschmitt Bf 110C Zerstörer aircraft were delivered from Germany in 1940, and tested at NII VVS (flown by Pyotr N. Stefanovskiy, Mikhail I. Tarakanovskiy and others) and LII (with Igor I. Shelest, Aleksei I. Grinchik and others at the controls). At NII VVS an optical flight-data recorder was installed. The Bf 110 was demonstrated at LII to (among others) Aleksandr A. Arkhangelskiy of Tupolev's OKB (it is an ironical fact that NKVD had accused Tupolev of selling his designs to the Germans — enabling Messerschmitt to build the Bf 110!).

Like the Bf 190E, the Bf 110C also got high values by the NII VVS test pilots. The max. speed was recorded to be 525 km/h at 4,600 m altitude and 442 km/h at ground level, climbing time to 5,000 m 8.4 minutes, and a full 360 degrees turn was made in 30 seconds. The fire power was even greater than that of the Bf 109E: the one-second burst equalled 2.85 kg.

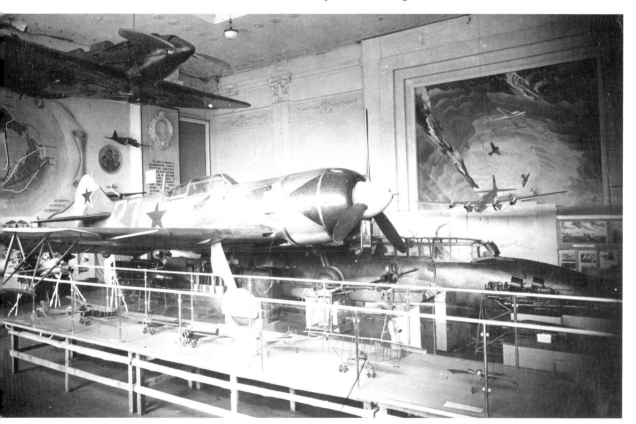

An interior view of the Frunze aviation museum in Moscow in the 1950s. In this context the Messerschmitt Bf 110 fuselage (first sign of the code is visible: 5_ + __) behind the much-publicized Lavochkin La-7 ("27") of the triple-HSU Ivan Kozhedub is of particular interest. The ultimate fate of the Bf 110 is unknown (as is that of the rare Polikarpov I-17 fighter hanging from the ceiling).

A Messerschmitt Bf 110 at
the war booty exhibition
in Moscow. The picture
seems to have been taken
in the late autumn 1944,
as the snow has already
fallen.

One of the Bf 110s delivered from Germany was also used as a flying testbed for the experimental 23 mm MP-6 cannon designed by Ya.G. Taubin and M.N. Baburin in 1940.

In September 1941 a Bf 110 was forced down by Ivan Ye. Plekhanov of the 158 IAP PVO (to become 103 Guards IAP on 7 July 1943) at the Leningrad front. This Bf 110 was taken to the regiment's main base, and extensively studied by the technical personnel, who called it "Ivan's laboratory" after its conqueror. There is however no indication of flight testing of this aircraft. (Plekhanov became a HSU on 28 January 1943.)

In winter 1942 a Bf 110 was used operationally by one long-range bomber regiment, the 750 AP DD (to become 3 Guards AP ADD on 18 August 1943). It was flown by Sen-Lt Vyacheslav G. Opalev and his co-pilot Yevgeni Okorokov, carrying out "free-hunting" operations in the German rear. An unsuspecting Junkers Ju 88 had already been shot down on the first mission. Opalev made a total of approximately 10 such clandestine operations with the Bf 110, before being shot down by his own AA fire at Tula. He was able to save his life by parachuting, but was killed in action in August 1943 at Kursk. The official ADD history indicates that Bf 110s (and other captured German aircraft) were also used by other ADD units for similar tasks, unfortunately without giving any further details.

A radar-equipped night-fighter Bf 110G-4/R-4 (G9 + AA, WNr 140655 of Stab/NJG 1) which had force-landed in Trelleborg, Sweden was delivered to USSR dismantled on 8 November 1945.

The two-seat Messerschmitt Me 163S was tested at LII (without engine power, as no fuel was available) in 1945-46 primarily by Mark L. Gallaj, being towed by a Tupolev Tu-2 piloted by his test-pilot colleague Igor I. Shelest. Note the LII emblem on both sides of the tail.

Messerschmitt Me 163

More than 20 Messerschmitt Me 163 rocket- and Me 262 jet-powered fighters were captured by Soviet forces at Oranienburg, Dalgow and Tempelhof in April-May 1945.

The two-seater Me 163 S (which had been captured intact at Brandis) was tested at LII (without engine power, as no fuel was available) in 1945-46 by Mark L. Gallaj, being towed by a Tupolev Tu-2 piloted by his test-pilot colleague Igor I. Shelest (it is an interesting coincidence that both Gallaj and Shelest have become well-known authors, with both publishing their reminiscences of the test-flying in several volumes of memoirs). One of the main tasks of the test programme was to establish whether jet aircraft could be safely landed without engine power. After a number of successful flights Gallaj had a narrow escape when crashing whilst landing after deliberately having moved the aircraft's centre of gravity. The Me 163 was damaged beyond repair, but Gallaj was able to continue the powerless flying in

The Messerschmitt Me 163B rocket fighter was tested at NII VVS by Vladimir Ye. Golofastov, with Ivan P. Piskunov piloting the Tu-2 towing aircraft. The Me 163 depicted may be WNr 191952, which is reported to have been captured by the Soviets.

another Me 163 after three weeks. Gallay writes: "the cockpit of the Me 163 had a certain 'German' smell which reminded me of the other Messerschmitt, Bücker and Junkers aircraft I had flown before." He told this author in 1983 that he was in fact disappointed that the Soviets had no rocket fuel available for the Me 163 — he would have been very eager to test the real potential of the rocket fighter.

The Me 163 S was also flown by the LII test pilots Yakov I. Vernikov (a former fighter ace with 16 victories, decorated with the HSU award 18 November 1944 as assistant commander of 147 Guards IAP) and A.A. Yefimov, while a one-seater was tested at NII VVS by Vladimir Ye. Golofastov, with Ivan P. Piskunov piloting the Tu-2 towing aircraft. This test was very troublesome as the take-off trolley release mechanism malfunctioned. At an altitude of 1000 m Golofastov was made aware of the situation by the Tu-2 crew. A decision was then taken to dive and try to release the trolley at low altitude. The towing cable however remained stuck to the trolley, and pulled the Me 163 upside down. Golofastov succeeded in turning his aircraft back to a normal position, but the same problem reappeared. Piskunov then decided to climb again, and the towing cable was released. Golofastov had to fly inverted 1½ turns and then make a 45 degree dive before landing successfully. He ultimately made a total of 17 flights from a maximum release altitude of 6000 m, performing the required tests in 5 minutes while the Me 163 dived to 2000 m, with the Tu-2 closely following.

The Soviet test-pilots Georgi K. Mosolov (HSU 5.10.1960), Valentin P. Vasin (HSU 1.5.1957) and Yuriy A. Garnayev (HSU 21.8.1964, killed in a Mi-6 helicopter accident, fighting a forest fire in France 6.8.1967) were later to develop methods to safely land jet-fighters without engine power, which has saved the lives of several Soviet fighter pilots in emergency situations.

The Messerschmitt Me 163S being towed to releasing altitude by the Tupolev Tu-2. Note the camera installation (?) above the cockpit.

The Mikoyan I-270 (Zh) rocket fighter designed in 1945 was clearly influenced by the Messerschmitt Me 163.

Messerschmitt Me 262

In the winter of 1944/45 the Messerschmitt Me 262 jet-fighter was encountered on a number of occasions by Soviet fighter pilots. Some victories over the Me 262 are reported, although there are some inconsistencies in the published accounts — and some reported Me 262 kills seem merely to be the result of wishful thinking.

The No 1 Soviet ace with 62 victories and triple-HSU (4.2.1944, 19.8.1944 and 18.8.1945), Maj. Ivan N. Kozhedub (176 Guards IAP; ex-19 IAP, made Guards on Aviation Day, 19 August 1944) with Maj. K. Titarenko as his wing-man shot down one Me 262 on 19 February 1945 (24 February according to another edition of Kozhedub's memoirs) in the Frankfurt-an-der-Oder area.

On 22 March 1945 L.I. Sivko (812 IAP) shot down an Me 262 in the Zechin area, being killed himself when his Yakovlev Yak-9 was hit by debris from the exploding Me 262.

Lt-Gen Yevgeni Ya. Savitskiy (CO 3 IAK) assisted by Maj P. Okolelov is also reported as scoring one Me 262 jet, which attacked a group of nine Soviet bombers in the Berlin area on 26 April, 1945. (According to another account Savitskiy was however not able to hit the much faster Me 262 — as was verified by his gun-camera.)

An Me 262 "kill" is also reported by Sen-Lt Garri A. Merkviladze (152 Guards IAP; ex-270 IAP). Finally, Capt. Ivan A. Kuznetsov (HSU 27.6.1945 with 10 victories), Sen-Lt P. Trofimov and Ltn V. Semyonov (107 Guards IAP, ex-867 IAP, which was made Guards on 25 August 1943) succeeded in downing an Me 262 flown by a "factory test pilot" on 30 April, 1945 in the Adlig-Dubran area.

That the Me 262 was considered a serious threat to the Soviet Air Force is evident from the fact that the 16th Air Army arranged a big conference at the end of February 1945 to discuss possible methods of fighting jets with conventional piston-engined aircraft. The conference was opened by Col-Gen Sergei I. Rudenko (CO 16th Air Army), and speeches were presented by Lt-Col A.I. Novikov (Deputy CO 3 IAK), Lt-Col V.M. Makarov (CO 176 Guards IAP; ex-240 IAP), Maj. Ivan N. Kozhedub (Deputy CO 176 Guards IAP; the conference took place a few days after Kozhedub's Me 262 victory), Maj. Ivan I. Kobyletskiy (Deputy CO of 53 Guards IAP; ex-512 IAP which was made Guards on 31 January 1943. Kobyletskiy received his HSU award on 15 May 1946 with 15 personal and 9 "group" victories) and Capt. Gennadi S. Dubenok (53 Guards IAP; HSU 24.8.1943).

It was pointed out to the participants that the speed superiority of the Me 262 as compared to the Soviet fighters was similar to the relative speed advantage of the Messerschmitt Bf 109 versus the Polikarpov I-16 at the beginning of the war in 1941 — and the Bf 109, could in numerous cases, be successfully shot down by I-16 pilots. Furthermore, the Me 262 was able to use its top speed only for very short dashes. In order to upset the German jet pilots it was recommended to open fire at distances of up to 600 m — even if the hit probability was nil (this recom-mendation shows clearly a bit of panic from the Soviets because of the German jet potential.)

As is already mentioned in the section on the Me 163 more than 20 Me 163s and Me 262s were captured in Oranienburg, Dalgow and Tempelhof by units of the 16th Air Army. Lt-Gen Savitskiy is reported to have eagerly studied the cockpit of one Me 262 in Dalgow, assisted by a German POW jet pilot.

A number of Me 262s were also found by the 2 Guards IAP (ex-526 IAP) at Schabindorf. Intact aircraft were carefully evacuated and studied by the specialists at NII VVS. The first Soviet pilot to fly the Me 262 jet fighter was Andrei G. Kochetkov of NII VVS on 15 August 1945 in an Me 262 which had been captured in East Prussia in April 1945. This aircraft had been repaired under supervision by the NII VVS Chief Engineer Izrail G. Rabkin. Kochetkov made a total of 18 flights in the Me 262 up to November 1945, and was awarded the HSU on 26 June 1958. The second Soviet airman to try the German jet was the NII VVS Chief Test-Pilot Pyotr N. Stefanovskiy on 30 October 1945. The Me 262 was also flown by Afanasiy G. Proshakov, Andrei G. Terentyev, Yevgeni Ya. Savitskiy and others.

When Kochetkov was given the task of establishing the maximum speed of the Me 262 (fortunately at the altitude of 11,000 m) the aircraft superstalled when reaching the speed of 870 km/h, and he had extreme difficulties in levelling off again. Using all his accumulated test-pilot experience he finally succeeded in regaining control of the aircraft. A captured German instructional film showing the difficult handling characteristics of the Me 262 later confirmed the negative experience of Kochetkov.

Former NII VVS test pilot Andrej Kochetkov describing his experiences of the Me 262 flight-testing to the author in summer 1983.

According to Western sources this Me 262 was WNr 170063 of *Ofw* Helmut Lennartz, JG 7, who crash-landed at Kolberg in April 1945. The engines had filled with earth during the belly-landing, hence the aircraft was not immediately serviceable. The reason for Kochetkov's troubles is further said to have been a malfunctioning trim control relay. This aircraft was later tested by the NII VVS test-pilot Fedor F. Demida, who crashed fatally on 17 September 1946 because of a defective engine ball-bearing. (Demida was the first jet pilot to be killed on duty at NII VVS.)

The Me 262 was however to be the subject of a major controversy in the Soviet aviation industry and air force, as a number of persons in influential positions voted for the start of Soviet production of an Me 262 copy, with others strongly opposing this idea. According to the memoirs of Aleksandr S. Yakovlev (then Deputy Minister of Aircraft Industry responsible for R&D) his superior, Minister Aleksei I. Shakhurin was the main supporter of the Me 262 production idea, while Yakovlev himself was a resolute opponent of the Me 262.

Yakovlev presented his arguments at a top level meeting with Stalin: "It is a bad aircraft, and difficult for the pilots to control, which is proved by a number of catastrophes in Germany. If it (ie the proposed Me 262 production) is accepted, our pilots will get an aversion against jet technology as they will soon realize by themselves that this is a dangerous aircraft with bad characteristics. Finally, if we are going to copy the Me 262, then all our attention will be directed towards this aircraft, which will obstruct the development of our own jet technology in a very negative way." Stalin's decision was in line with Yakovlev's proposal, concentrating the efforts on developing Mikoyan's MiG-9 and Yakovlev's own Yak-15 jet fighters which were considered more promising than the Me 262. (*See* the section on

The Messerschmitt Me 262 jet fighter was tested at NII VVS, its first flight with "red stars" being performed on 15 August 1945 by A.G. Kochetkov.

He 162 for the joint demonstration of the "*Volkjäger*" and the Soviet prototypes on 11 July 1946. It is unknown whether or not the Me 262 was also demonstrated in the air on this occasion — and if not, then why not?)

The Me 262 controversy led to the dismissal (and later imprisonment) of Shakhurin. It is easy to see that — apart from any rational arguments — any supporter of German, ie enemy technology would *a priori* be politically suspect. Mikhail V. Khrunishev was appointed as Shakhurin's successor as Minister of Aviation Industry. Shakhurin was released from prison and fully rehabilitated only after Stalin's death in 1953. He even returned to his former Ministry working for some time as Deputy Minister, subordinated to his former junior Pyotr V. Dementyev! Shakhurin died on 3 June 1975.

Yakovlev also left (voluntarily?) the office of Deputy Minister as a result of this conflict, concentrating on proving his arguments, ie finalizing the design of the Yak-15.

(It is symptomatic that Shakhurin does not say a word about the events leading to his dismissal in his memoirs, published posthumously in 1983. Furthermore, his references to Yakovlev are rather few in number. Not even the new, expanded and advertised as "unexpurgated" edition published in 1990 gives any additional information on these intriguing events.)

Note: The former People's Commissariats had been renamed Ministries in connection with a reform of the Soviet governmental administration in March 1946.

It is a noteworthy fact that the issue of copying the Boeing B-29 Superfortress (which was approvingly decided!) must have been handled by Stalin at approximately the same time as the Me 262 production was being discussed (if not even at the same conference!).

It was however decided to start Soviet production of German jet engines which were considered superior to the comparable Soviet projects. The Junkers Jumo 004 was thus produced as the RD-10 (to be used in the Yak-15) and the BMW 003 as the RD-20 (used in the MiG-9).

The Messerschmitt Me 410A-2/U4 being tested at NII VVS. Note the 50 mm BK 5 cannon (modified KWK 39 tank gun).

Messerschmitt Me 410

The two-engine Me 410 was the last German piston-engine fighter to be fully tested at NII VVS during the war. The tests of the 50 mm cannon-equipped Me 410B-2 (WNr 130379) were however completed only after V-E day. The heavy cannon (total weight 592 kg compared to the take-off weight of the aircraft 10,410 kg) impaired however the performance of the aircraft rather considerably. The high-performance aiming system enabled the pilot to use his cannon efficiently even from a distance of 1000 m. The Me 410 was considered a dangerous opponent for the Tu-2 and Pe-2 bombers, which it could easily outspeed, and was also astonishingly manoeuvrable and a stable gun-platform. Against the fast Soviet fighters it could however only perform defensively.

Siebel Si 204

A number of Siebel Si 204 twin-engined light transports were used by *Polarnaya Aviatsiya* after the war, flown by Matvey I. Kozlov, and others including even Maj-Gen Vasili I. Stalin (the Soviet dictator's son!). He commanded 32 Guards IAP, 3 Guards IAD (ex-210 IAD, Guards on 17 March 1943) and finally 286 IAD at the end of the Second World War). That he had personally piloted the Siebel aircraft is certified in his official *Curriculum Vitae* signed 7 July 1946 by Lt-Gen Yevgeni Ya. Savitskiy (CO 3 IAK).

The Siebel flown by Vasili Stalin was probably the VIP-courier aircraft at the disposal of Savitskiy's IAK in Germany. Savitskiy even flew it himself, and liked its ample instrumentation very much as it enabled safe blind flying. Savitskiy was to utilize all capacities of his courier aircraft when he was given the task by Marshal G.S. Zhukov himself to transport an extremely important passenger from Dalgow to Marshal Konev in Praha, Czechoslovakia, in the summer of 1945. The identity of the VIP-passenger — who was seen off at the airport by Marshal Zhukov himself — was not revealed to Savitskiy and his crew (Maj. L. Novikov and Lt. Gladkov). Regardless of an extremely bad weather forecast they decided to do their utmost to fulfil Marshal Zhukov's order, which required a landing practically in darkness at the Praha airport — not equipped for night operations! After a very difficult flight they succeeded in landing at Praha, where Savitskiy reported to Marshal Konyev, and asked for permission to return to Dalgow the following morning. Konyev did not give his permission, however, but instead granted Savitskiy the day off and "ordered" him to go to the Stadium to watch the soccer game between TsSKA (the Red Army team) and one of the best English soccer teams. It turned out that Savitskiy's secret VIP was the goal-keeper urgently needed by Konyev's team . . . (The match was won by the Red Army, so Savitskiy's efforts had not been in vain!)

Note: And what happened to Vasili Stalin? He spent some time in East Germany, touring German aviation and missile factories (*see* Postscript), in July 1947 he was appointed Assistant to the CO of the Air Force of the Moscow Military District, and on 18 July 1948 was appointed CO of this Air Force as a Lt.-General when only 27 years old. He was most of all still very interested in soccer, and also in drinking with "friends", who through him tried to gain access to the Soviet dictator. He was, however, relieved of his command by his father after the May Day parade in 1952, when a number of participating aircraft crashed, and Vasili was held responsible for the unsatisfactory preparations.

As it became known that Vasili had been behind the repressions of the wartime CO Soviet AF Marshal Aleksandr A. Novikov and the former Minister of Aircraft Industry Aleksandr Shakkurin (*see* Me 262 section), none of the professional aviators seem to have regretted his fate. After the Soviet dictator's death on 5 March 1953, Vasili was kicked out of the Soviet Army, without even the right to carry his uniform! From this time on, his life was very tragic – in and out of prisons for various reasons. He took even more to the bottle, and he spent many sessions in alcoholic sanatoriums until he died on 19 March 1962, virtually forgotten and unknown. He is buried in Kazan, where he lived out his last years. The simple inscription on his grave reads, *Dzhugashvili Vasili Iosifovich 24.3.1920–19.3.1962*. (Dzhugashvili was the original Georgian surname of Stalin.)

A Czechoslovak-built Siebel Si 204 (post-war Czechoslovak designation C-3) being tested at NII GVF (Civil Aviation Research Institute) 1945.

A Siebel Si 204 of AVIAARKTIKA (note inscription!) at Igarka (not far from the mining centre of Norilsk) at the Yenisej river.

A Siebel Si 204 at Khorog (at the mountainous border between the Tadzhikskaya SSR and Afghanistan) in 1946.

The Siebel Si 204 also flew with Soviet civil registrations CCCP N-35_ in the picture.

"EVACUATION" OF THE ROCKET AND AIRCRAFT INDUSTRY FROM EAST GERMANY

1. Rocket technology

At the end of the war the Soviets naturally became extremely interested in the German jet and rocket technology. In September 1944 a German test facility for the V-2 missiles at Dembidze, near Krakow, Poland was captured. Before retreating the Germans had tried to destroy all traces of the rocket testing. Only by air photography were the Soviet specialists able to trace the location of the facilities, and some rocket parts were located by engineers urgently sent for from Moscow. The parts were loaded on a Lisunov Li-2 bound for the Soviet capital where they were to be investigated, but according to Gen. Stepan A. Krasovskiy (1897-1983; commanded 2nd and 17th Air Armies during the war) "the aircraft crashed at Kiyev and all parts burned". However, some V-2 parts did reach Moscow and the NII-1 (ex-RNII). The Deputy Director of NII-1 was V.F. Bolkhovitinov, who had been occupied with the design of liquid-fuelled rocket engines during the war. He immediately formed a group of talented scientists to examine the burned rocket parts: N.A. Pilyugin, A.Ya. Bereznyak, B.Ye. Chertov, L.A. Voskresenskyj, V.P. Mishin, M.K. Tikhonravov, Yu.A. Pobedonostsev, Bordachev, Borovikov, Konovalov and Frolov. The Chief Designer of a rocket-fuelled engine OKB, Aleksej M. Isayev (1908-71), told in his reminiscences how he participated in the reconstruction and analysis of a V-2, from burned parts recovered in Poland, at a rocket NII in autumn 1944. (Isayev had already in 1942 designed the first Soviet rocket-powered aircraft, the BI-1 together with Aleksandr Ya. Bereznyak, who was eg. to work as "co-director" of the German OKB-2 in the Soviet Union from 1946; *see* Chapter 5.)

It turned out later that the Germans had relocated a major part of their rocket experiments from Peenemünde to Dembidze after the major allied bombings of Peenemünde in 1943. According to Soviet sources, when the Western allies became aware of the Soviet capture of the facilities at Dembidze, Churchill repeatedly asked Stalin for permission to send British rocket specialists to take part in the investigations at Dembidze. The Soviet specialists at NII-1 made calculations of the trajectories and aerodynamical parameters of the V-2, reconstructed its general configuration etc. Based on the reconstructed data, a proposal to design a modernized version of the V-2 was made. The analysis and corresponding proposals were presented in November 1944 to the top level of the aviation industry: People's Commissar A.I. Shakhurin and his Deputy P.V. Dementyev. The decision was astonishingly negative: rockets are no concern of the aviation industry, but these "toys" will be handled by the Ministry of Munitions, where the "Stalin's organs", the famous "*Katyushas*" were being produced. According to a recent interview with Vasili P. Mishin this unfounded and unwise decision led to the still existing invisible barrier between aircraft and missile development in Russia, which recently hampered eg. the development of the Soviet space shuttle "*Buran*", which apparently never will make a manned flight! The lack of understanding shown from the Ministry of Aviation even led to the dissolution of Bolkhovitinov's expert team. However, on "his own risk" he instructed Mishin to continue the design calculations of high altitude and long-distance rockets based on the analysis of the V-2 parts. As the future would show, this decision would turn out to be a most far-sighted one!

Even before the end of the war the Soviets planned special expert commissions to follow immediately behind the advancing Red Army into Germany. The commissions were directed by the future Soviet Prime Minister Georgiy M. Malenkov (1902-88, member of the State Defense Committee, 1941-45. In late 1943 he was appointed Chairman of a Government Committee, the task of which was to restore the national economy in the Soviet areas which had been occupied by Germany). The task was to prevent the destruction of the German armament factories and secure the capture of the personnel, equipment and documentation of the scientific institutes and R&D departments in the territory occupied by the Soviet forces. A virtual competition for German scientists and engineers between the Soviets and the Western powers (which had initiated their well-known "Operation Paperclip") began. However, after denying the German ancestry of their rocket technology for decades, the Russians now admit regretfully that the Western allies were better prepared for the collection and assimilation of this new technology. In many cases war-tired Soviet military commanders seem to have lost the possibility to secure valuable information because of sheer incompetence or bureaucratic quarrels, concentrating only on collecting conventional war-booty, and not understanding the value of, eg. the German nuclear and rocket research.

The main aviation specialist at the "*Soviet Military Administration of Germany*" (ie the Soviet occupation administration of East Germany headed by Marshal Grigoriy M. Zhukov) was Lt-Gen Timofej F. Kutsevalov (1904-75, HSU 17.11.1939 as CO of 56 IAP at Khalkhin-Gol, where he scored 4 personal and 5 shared victories. During the war he had commanded, ie the Air Force of the North-Western and Western Fronts, 12 Air Army etc). At his side he had (in addition to the inevitable security officers) both permanent and temporarily assigned air force engineers and scientists. Maj-Gen Vasili Stalin (the dictator's son who at the end of the war commanded the 286 IAD) also personally took an active part in the study of

German aviation technology. Kutsevalov's Deputy was Professor Grigoriy A. Tokayev (of the Zhukovskiy Air Force Engineering Academy in Moscow) who later defected to the west. Tokayev's candid memoirs published in the 1950s gave a unique insight into the occupation administration and aviation policy of the Soviet Union, but were obviously not given the attention they deserved!

Tokayev's memoirs have lately been partially confirmed by information published in the Soviet Union during the *Glasnost* period.

Concerning access to the the German aeronautics know-how potential, the Soviet Union was in a favourable position, as up to two thirds of the German aircraft factories were located in what was to become the Soviet occupation zone:

— Siebel, Halle
— Heinkel, Rostock-Warnemünde and Oranienburg
— Junkers, Dessau
— Messerschmitt, Wiener Neustadt
— Arado, Berlin-Babelsberg
— Dornier, Wismar
— Henschel, Erfurt and Berlin

The most important aircraft engine factories were also captured by the Soviets:

— Junkers-Motoren-Werke, Bernburg an der Saale
— BMW, Eisenach

On 24 May 1945 the first group of Soviet rocket specialists flew to Berlin. This commission was headed by Gen. L.M. Gajdukov (director of a department of the CPSU Central Committee), his Deputies were A.I. Semenov and A.G. Mrykin. The commission included two specialists from the foremost rocket research institute NII-1 Dr Yu.A. Pobedonostsev and Vasili S. Budnik (later academician, formerly worked at the Ilyushin OKB), other members being Shapiro, Timofeyev and Volfovich. The commission toured Peenemünde, and examined the remains of the underground V-2 assembly plant, V-1 and V-2 launch sites etc. A surprise for the Soviet scientists was the multitude of different German rocket projects — including various missiles like *"Rheintochter"*, *"Rheinboth"*, *"Wasserfall"* and *"Taifun"*. At Peenemünde the Russians tried to assemble V-2 rockets from parts with the assistance of German "volunteers". As Budnik explained in an interview in 1991 a total of ten V-2s were partly assembled, but with "moderate success only". After this all available documentation was collected and translated into Russian. The commission moved back to Berlin, and then further on to Nordhausen in Thuringia, where one of the main German rocket and missile factories was located in underground salt mines.

In August 1945 a new, technically more competent group of people arrived by a Lisunov Li-2 passenger aircraft in Germany to assist the commission. The newcomers included a number of specialists of future world fame: Sergey P. Korolev (1907-66; he was to become the anonymous Chief Designer of the Soviet spacecraft and intercontinental missiles, with his identity revealed only after his death. At the end of the 1930s he had been a convict in the same "engineers' prison" as Andrey N. Tupolev.), Valentin P. Glushko (1908- ; future responsible designer of the rocket engines of Korolev's spacecraft), Nikolay A. Pilyugin (1908-82; future designer of control systems of Soviet spacecraft), Vasily P. Barmin (1909- ; future head of construction of the Baikonur Space Centre, and still in 1989 in overall control of the *Buran* space shuttle project), Vasiliy P. Mishin (to become Korolev's Deputy, and later to be appointed Chief Constructor) and Lt-Gen Georgiy A. Tyulin (future Chairman of the State Commission for cosmonautics and spacecraft), M.S. Ryazanskij (future Corresponding member of the Academy of Sciences), Boguslavskij, V.A. Rudnitskij, Florenskij, Bakurin and Goryunov, who all eagerly studied the V-2 rockets in every detail. This group — partly consisting of members like Korolev whose reliability was questioned — arrived in Germany under even stricter secrecy than the main commission arriving in May. The members of Korolev's group had been summoned one by one to the CPSU Central Committee only the day before, and had been told only that they were to leave for East Germany on the next day as members of a secret Interdepartmental mission. The task of their "business" trip was not revealed before arrival in Berlin on 9 August 1945. In order not to raise unnecessary questions they were all given military ranks — Colonel or Lt-Col. The scientists were thus jokingly named "the Colonels" among themselves. The Senior Lieutenant Budnik was correspondingly also made a Lt-Col which caused some astonished reaction from some of his East German aquaintancies when they saw his new shoulder straps: "Herr Bubnik — what a fast career you have made!"

The multitude of information collected in various places soon required the set-up of a special office for documentation collection and restoration. In Berlin an exhibition of rocket technology was organized, and even production and assembly of V-2 rockets at the Rheinmetall-Borsig factory was scheduled to be reopened. The foundation of a joint German-Soviet documentation restoration centre was also planned, when the Soviet scientists were informed that a railway truck full of rocket drawings to be dispatched to Austria had been captured by Czechoslovak insurgent forces near Prague! A group led by V.M. Mishin was immediately sent via Nordhausen to Prague to investigate the drawings. In Nordhausen some Soviet scientists led by B.Ye. Chertok and A.M. Isayev were already investigating the former underground V-2 factory. Mishin could only note regretfully that his colleagues occupied the former villa of Werner von Braun, but the former master had already irreversibly escaped to the west . . . In Prague the Russian scientists were able to locate the German V-2 production co-ordination office, which had directed all supply of subassemblies and parts from hundreds of companies in Austria, Hungary, Poland and Czechoslovakia, in addition to Germany proper. But the technical documentation was still missing . . . As the Anglofile Benes administration was not very willing to assist the Soviets, Mishin had to "apply unorthodox measures" and after some cat-and-mouse adventures (where a significant part was played by the sister of A.Ya. Bereznyak who had been imprisoned in a German concentration camp) he was able to secure the missile documentation. The thorough investigation by Mishin showed however that the V-2 documentation was still far from complete. Under his supervision an office was organized at Bleicherode near Nordhausen where the Russian scientists continued the theoretical analysis of the V-2 design. Mishin's former calculations, based on the investigation of the burned parts secured in Poland, soon enabled him to fill the gaps, and he was obviously able to tell his superiors that now the Russians were in possession of virtually everything needed. The truck with the rocket documentation was subsequently directed to Moscow together with some gifts of the Czechoslovak government for Stalin: a Tatra limousine and some boxes of Pilzen beer. After this all Soviet rocket R&D activity was gradually relocated to Kaliningrad in the Moscow area. In this connection the Soviet rocket R&D was finally formally organized, and put under the supervision of the strong D.F. Ustinov — a future Defence Minister, and during the war People's Commissar for Armament.

It is common belief that Ustinov's first and only choice for the technical project leader was Korolev. According to Mishin, this was not the fact, as there was considerable political resistance against the appointment of the former convict Korolev, and S. Sinel'shchikov, who worked with the "*Wasserfall*" anti-aircraft rockets in Germany was the first choice. After some consideration Korolev was however appointed.

In order to perform test launches of the V-2 in Germany a special joint Soviet-German group with the code name "*Vystrel*" (Shot) was soon organized by Korolev. However, the Germans available to him were unfortunately only "second-hand" specialists, as all the major designers like von Braun were already in the west. The most important German V-2 expert working for the Russians was G. Gertrud. In the British occupation sector similar investigations into the German rocket technology were carried out, and as the "cold war" between the former allies had not yet broken out, the British even invited the Russians to watch a V-2 launch in the Hamburg area. Among the Russians attending was Korolev with a false passport. (This was obviously Korolev's only personal contact with Western colleagues. During his "active" years as the General Designer of the Soviet spacecraft, his identity was never revealed, and he was not allowed to travel abroad, nor to meet any foreign representatives!)

As a result of this successful British launch Korolev's group was reorganized as the "*Nordhausen*" institute, and put under direct military command with Gen. O.M. Gajdukov as CO with Korolev as his Deputy.

Soon after a high-level Soviet military-technical commission led by Marshal of Artillery N.D. Yakovlev, and including among others D.F. Ustinov visited East Germany in order to review the progress of the various R&D teams analyzing the German armament technology.

Subordinated to the *"Nordhausen"* Institute a joint Soviet-German OKB led by V.P. Mishin was now organized at Zommers near Erfurt, the task of which was to, based on the former theoretical analysis, produce complete technical and manufacturing documentation of the V-2 as soon as possible. The rocket propulsion subteam was led by V.P. Glushko, the control subgroup by N. A. Pilyugin, V.I. Kuznetsov and B.Ye. Chertok, with the ground equipment subgroup by B.P. Barmin.

Already in 1946 Soviet rocket launches from Peenemünde were subsequently reported in the Swedish press — and presumably confirmed by American intelligence.

Meanwhile the State Commission had decided to relocate the rocket R&D and assembly of V-2s from German parts to USSR. A special design bureau NII-88 led by Korolev, with Mishin as his Deputy, heading the Computational Department and Budnik the Design Department, was thus set up at Podlipki, north of Moscow, now better known as Kaliningrad. After exactly one year in East Germany Mishin returned to Moscow on 9 August 1946. The main task of NII-88 was to initiate production of the V-2 and the *"Wasserfall"* in the Soviet Union. The first batch of "Soviet V-2s", code-named *"product T"* was assembled from parts brought from Germany. In addition to the production documentation and the rocket parts, spares and separate rocket instruments and systems, a number of complete V-2 rockets were also dispatched from East Germany to Russia.

Korolev himself returned from Germany to Podlipki at the end of February 1947, with the task of organizing the first launching of a V-2 rocket in the USSR. This first launching of a German V-2 rocket in the Soviet Union took place on 18 October 1947 at the test range at Kapustin Yar. At this time there were virtually no facilities at *"Kap.Yar"* as it was named for short by the Russian scientists, so they had to live and work in two trains standing nearby to the launch site (which was later to become one of the world-famous Soviet "Cosmodromes"). The first launch could have ended in a catastrophe, as it went beyond control, heading in the direction of the city of Saratov! After correction of the control system a total of eleven V-2 launches were made in USSR.

A number of other deficiencies of the German design were also detected during the tests, and these were gradually corrected. The next batch of rockets was assembled from parts manufactured in the Soviet Union according to the original German documentation. Gradually the "Sovietization" of the V-2 made progress, and Korolev was soon busy developing a Soviet rocket family (R-1A, R-1B, R-1V, R-1D and R-1E) based on the German V-2. According to Budnik, the main difference between the original V-2 and the Soviet R-1 was a completely new control and guidance system resulting in considerable improved overall reliability. After less than one year the first pure Soviet R-1 rocket was launched from Kapustin Yar on 10 October 1948, with a maximum range of 270 kilometres.

After this success the design bureau OKB-1 was formed at NII-88, with the main task of increasing the range of the R-1 rocket to 600 km. The fuselage construction of the V-2 could however not stand the increased range. After thorough theoretical investigation of the two different phases of the V-2 flight envelope — the first actively-powered flight, and the second, ballistic, after engine burn-out — a decision was taken to separate the warhead from the main rocket carrier after burn-out of the engines, which turned out to solve all problems. The new rocket was named R-2, and became the ancestor of all Soviet strategic missiles. When the series production of the R-2 was planned the capacity of the Kaliningrad factory was unsufficient, so the construction of a new specialized missile factory, based on an existing car plant at Dnepropetrovsk in the Ukraine, was planned. The Dnepropetrovsk factory was disguisingly named "*Yushnyj mashinostroitelnyj zavod*" (Southern machinebuilding factory) with the attached design bureau "*Yuzhnoye*". The enormous "Southern" Design Bureau and Factory (whose existences were only recently revealed) have been responsible for the design and production of almost all Soviet ICBMs.

Tokayev also describes the great personal interest Stalin himself took in the plans of Dr Eugen Sänger (of *Deutsche Forschungsanstalt für Segelflug*) to construct a manned supersonic intercontinental bomber, and the means undertaken to catch Sänger. However, Sänger was already in the west and unreachable for the Soviets.

Professor Kurt Tank was also offered the opportunity to work for the Soviets after the war and continue the development of his jet aircraft projects (Tokayev mentions explicitly the Ta-183 and Ta-185 fighter and the Ta-900 bomber projects). Because of unbelievable bureaucratic confusion the negotiations held with Tank in 1947 in East Germany (according to Tokayev's unbiased account it seems that real negotiations were in question, and the Soviets did — somewhat unexpectedly — not threaten to use force on him!) were interrupted, and he never did get on the Moscow plane that was waiting for him and Tank was subsequently able to return West. As is well-known he continued his career as jet aircraft designer in Argentina, Spain, Egypt and India.

2. Aircraft technology

In 1945 in the Soviet-occupied East Germany the Soviets organized the remaining aircraft designers and specialists into two OKBs according to the Soviet model, in order to maximize the utilization and transfer of the know-how of the former German aircraft companies.

Relocation of these OKBs to the USSR was rather soon deemed necessary in order to achieve the results wanted, and thus the bulk of the German scientists and engineers working in the two Soviet-controlled OKBs were, without any previous warning, put on trains with their families to the Soviet Union on the night between 22 and 23 October 1946, together with documentation, scientific equiment and technical material.

According to eyewitnesses' accounts, even the complete working environment of the German specialists was removed to the USSR. Accommodation was rather primitive compared to German standards, but was considered very good by the Russians. The aircraft designers and engineers were located at the Aircraft factory No. 256 at Podberezye, near Dubna, approx. 150 km north of Moscow at the so-called Moskovskoye more (Moscow Sea), and later relocated to aircraft factory No. 491 at Kimry in 1953.

The German aviation engine technology was also further developed under guidance by Dipl.-Ing. Ferdinand Brandner who had been one of the leading specialists of the Junkers engine works (*Otto-Mader-Werke*) at Dessau. Brandner worked at first at the engine factory No. 16 at Chernigovsk (near Ufa) headed by Nikolay D. Kuznetsov (1911-), and later at engine factory No. 19 in Kuibyshev where the entire Junkers/Dessau engine works had meanwhile been relocated. The German designers led by Brandner were first ordered to adopt the Jumo 004 jet engine (produced as RD-10 at engine factory No. 10 in Kazan) and the 3000 hp Jumo 222 double-V combustion engine for production in the USSR, before they were ordered to concentrate on turboprop engine development. This work was eventually to lead to the 15,000 hp turboprop engine NK-12 (for Nikolay Kuznetsov!) powering eg. the Tupolev Tu-114 "*Rossiya*" and the Antonov An-22 "*Antey*".

According to a carefully-worded Soviet reference to German jet propulsion technology, the well-known engine designer Aleksandr A. Mikulin (1895-), whose OKB had been evacuated to the engine factory at Kuibyshev, was given the task of examining some war-booty Jumo 004 and BMW 003 jet engines, and also rocket engines from V-1 and V-2 missiles at the end of the war. Mikulin found especially the Jumo 004 basic design very primitive, but equipped with a complicated control system. He was soon given the task of designing an indigenous jet engine in competition with A.M. Lyulka's OKB, to be used in "a concrete aircraft", while N.D. Kuznetsov's OKB was ordered to create engines based on "war trophy (ie. Ferdinand Brandner's!) designs". However, at the end of 1946 the Yakovlev Yak-15 jet fighter prototype equipped with an original Jumo jet engine was tested in the natural-size T-104 wind tunnel at TsAGI. The series-produced Yak-15s were already equipped with the Soviet-produced Jumo copy RD-10.

A similar enforced "technology transfer" of the BMW engine designs was also organized in the USSR, with the BMW 003 jet engine going into Soviet production as RD-20 at engine factory No. 466 "*Krasnyi Oktyabr*" in Leningrad.

The German aircraft designers were likewise at first ordered to finish such projects already started in Germany during the war, and which interested their new Soviet "masters" before they were given new tasks.

At the end of 1946 the Germans at Podberezye were organized into two OKBs:

OKB-1: Chief Designer Dr Brunolf Wilhelm Baade (former Chief Designer at the *Junkers Flugzeug-und Motorenwerke AG* in Dessau), with the Russian Pyotr N. Obrubov as his Deputy (and "supervisor").

OKB-2 led by Hans Heinrich Rössing (formerly with Siebel in Halle), with Aleksandr Ya. Bereznyak (1912-74; who had already constructed the first Soviet rocket aircraft BI-1 in 1942 together with the engine designer Aleksey M. Isayev; 1908-71, who was later to design rocket engines of several Soviet spacecraft) as the "Deputy" of Rössing. At OKB-2 the structural design department was led by Dipl.-Ing. Heinson, and the engine department by Dipl.-Ing. Schepp.

The German designers "employed" in the Soviet Union also included Dr Siegfried Günther (chief aerodynamician of the Heinkel company, who had made the general design of the *Volksjäger*, the Heinkel He 162 jet fighter in only four weeks in 1944) and Dr Benz (also an ex-Heinkel designer); Dipl.Ing. Hans Wocke and Dr Scheibe from the Junkers company etc.

The German test-pilots in the USSR included two ex-Junkers pilots, Dülgen and Hoffmann, and the former chief test-pilot of the Siebel factory, Wolfgang Ziese.

OKB-1 was given the task of continuing the Junkers jet-bomber design projects, while OKB-2 dealt with supersonic rocket-powered aircraft.

As these "German" OKBs in the Soviet Union were kept completely separated from not only the main Soviet OKBs but also from each other, with even strict internal security separation of the various departments of each OKB, the work was not very efficient as normal technical "diffusion of information" was completely excluded. As a Soviet comment says: "they were cooking in their own water. . ." This fact has furthermore initiated a great number of divergent rumours concerning the output of these OKBs as very few — if any — of the Germans were in the position to get an overview of the entire situation.

In 1948 Semyon M. Alekseyev (1900-60; during the war Deputy of Semyon A. Lavochkin). In 1946-48 Alekseyev was Chief Designer of the Aircraft Factory No. 21, where he designed a number of jet fighter prototypes, ie. the Gloster Meteor-resembling I-211 and I-215) was appointed joint Chief Designer of both German OKBs, with the task of co-ordinating the "German" projects with those of the main Soviet OKBs.

The following aircraft were designed at *OKB-1*:

EF-126: A one-seater experimental fighter powered by an Argus As 044 pulse-jet. Under development at the end of the war in Germany. A total of five unpowered prototypes were produced in Dessau before the transfer to the USSR. Completed and tested in the Soviet Union in 1947 "without any particular success". The EF-126 was intended to be used as a ground-attack aircraft (armed with *Panzerblitz*- or *Panzerschreck*-armament).

EF-131: A jet-powered bomber with six Jumo 004 engines (in two clusters of three engines each) and forward-swept wings. Development of the Junkers Ju 287, the second prototype (V2) which was finished at Dessau and tested in 1946 before it was transported to Russia and flight-tested in October 1946 by the German test-pilot Dülgen at Podberezye and Ramenskoye. The Ju 287 V3 was extensively used for static loading tests at TsAGI. The Ju 287 derivative EF-131 was transported incomplete to the USSR in autumn 1946 after extensive ground testing in East Germany in summer 1976. The EF 131V1 was flight tested by Dülgen at Podberezye. Further testing was taken over by Soviet teams. The project was cancelled in 1947.

EF-132: A giant jet bomber (take-off weight 100 tons!) with six Mikulin-developed jet engines (5000 kp thrust each). Originally planned for Jumo 012 engines. Wing swept 35 degrees. Prototype production planned, but cancelled in 1948 (only mock-up produced).

Type "140" (or *EF 140*): a twin-engined bomber, intended for Mikulin AM-1 engines. Chief designer G.N. Nazarov. The EF 140 prototype was in fact the rebuilt EF 131V1. Because of delays with the Soviet engines, the prototype had to be redesigned for Rolls-Royce *Nene* engines, leading to lack of the estimated performance. First test flight made by a German crew after which Soviet pilots took over. Development work cancelled in 1948.

Type "150": A twin-engined bomber intended to fulfil a VVS specification for an intermediate aircraft to fill the gap between Ilyushin Il-28 and Tupolev Tu-16. The main requirements of the specification were normal take-off weight 38 tons, max take-off weight 47 tons, velocity at ground level 790 km/h, at 5,000 m 970 km/h, max. altitude 12,500 m, and with a range between 1,500 and 4,500 km (depending on the bomb load). The "150" was powered by Lyulka AL-5 engines (5,000 kp thrust). Flight tested from May 1951. The "150" design incorporated a number of Soviet "firsts": eg. bicycle-type undercarriage and jet engines attached to underwing pylons, resulting in considerably bigger lift coefficient for equal air resistance, with the steeply forward-swept engine pylons acting as anti-flutter balances. Sixteen test flights were performed from May 1951, the prototype crashlanding on the sixteenth flight 9 May 1952 (test-pilot Yakov I. Vernikov, who had already flown the Messerschmitt Me 163S). Although the flights had confirmed that the "150" would fulfil the VVS requirements (recorded velocity at ground level 850 km/h against calculated 790 km/h, and 930 km/h at 10,000 m) it was decided to discontinue the development of the "150" after the crash of the prototype, as the need for an intermediate bomber was no more existing. The remains of the crashed prototype were handed over to the *Moskovskiy aviatsionnyy institut* (MAI) to be used in the laboratory of aircraft engineering. TsAGI participation (the efforts of the scientists V.N. Belyayev, A.I. Makarevskiy, the future Director-General of TsAGI G.P. Svishshev and S.A. Kristianovskiy are mentioned) in developing the aerodynamic configuration was substantial.

In a biography of the Soviet engine designer Boris S. Stechkin (1891-1969; who worked together with the space-craft designer Sergey P. Korolev during the last years of his life), written in 1978 by Feliks I. Chuyev, a spurious reference to Type "150" can be found:

"... a jet engine developed by B.S. Stechkin was intended for the jet aircraft designed by Baade, former Chief Engineer of the Junkers company. BAADE ARRIVED IN THE USSR FROM GERMANY AFTER THE WAR (emphasis here)... His aircraft was tested by Sazonov, and showed good characteristics, reaching a speed of 900 km/h."

Type "152": This was a transport derivative of Type "150", two prototypes being produced in the German Democratic Republic, after the "return" of *OKB-1* to East Germany in May 1956. The intention was to build-up a powerful aviation industry in East Germany, based on the experience and know-how collected in the USSR. The first prototype (DM-ZYA) made its initial flight on 4 December 1958. As the intended four Type 014A-0 axial-flow turbojets developed by *VEB Flugzeugwerke*

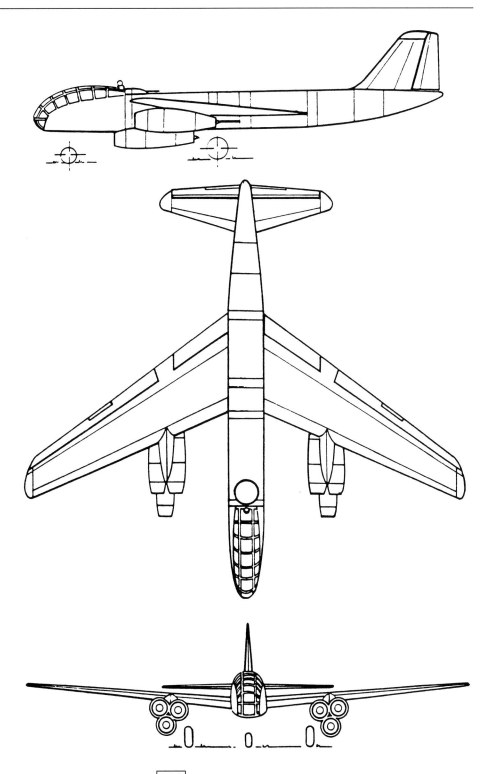

The six-engined EF 131
jet bomber was derived
from the Junkers Ju 287
and flight-tested in the
Soviet Union in 1946.

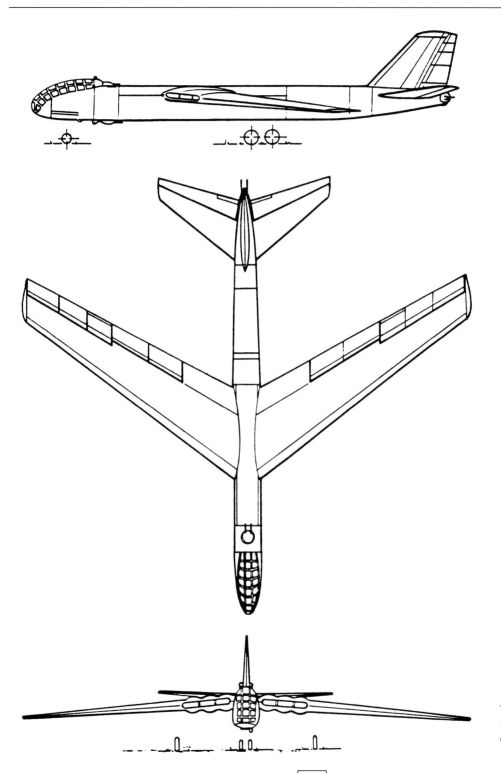

The design of the giant
EF 132 was continued in
OKB-1 but cancelled in
1948.

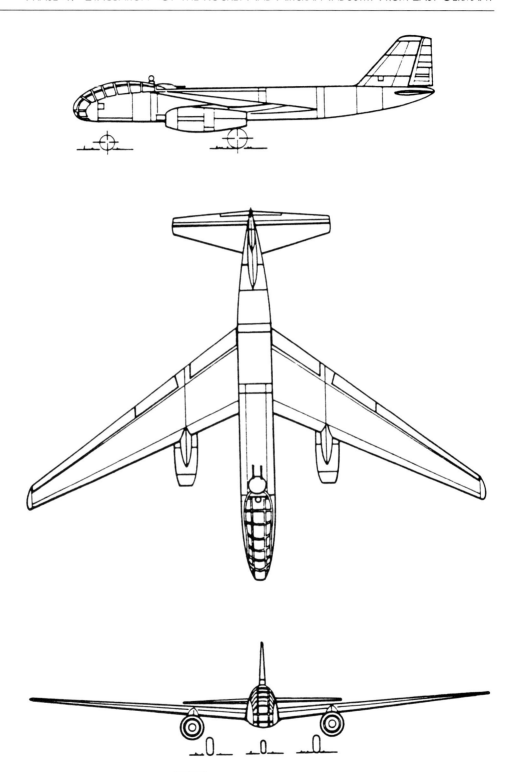

According to German sources the twin-jet EF 140 was also flight-tested: Soviet sources are however more vague with regard to the status of the project when cancelled in 1948.

at Pirna were not yet available, the prototype was powered by Soviet-made Mikulin RD-9B engines. This aircraft crashed near Leipzig on its second flight because of engine trouble. The brave intention was to make a demonstration flight (after one single flight only!) in front of the Soviet CPSU Secretary General Nikita S. Khrushchev, then in Leipzig on an official visit on 4 March 1959. After extensive development work the heavily-modified next prototype, the 152V4 (DM-ZYB) made its first flight on 26 August 1960 powered by East German Pirna 014A engines. It made its second and last flight on 4 September 1960. A total of seven prototypes were constructed, of which only V1 and V4 took off from the ground. The first flight of V5 was planned for 7 September 1960 but was cancelled. As it was realized that the Baade concept would never make a competitive airliner, the ambitious Baade "152" programme was entirely cancelled as unsuccessful on 5 April 1961, after enormous amounts of scarce resources had been spent. The crash of the Baade "152" led in fact to the end of the aircraft industry in the GDR.

In *OKB-2* two supersonic aircraft were designed, with a design target of 1.5 — 2.0 Mach.

The first one was the *Type 346* (DFS-346, also called "*Viktoriya*" in the USSR) powered by two Walther HWK 109-509 liquid-fuel rocket engines with a total thrust of 3740 kp at ground level, and 4000 kp at altitude. This was a one-seater all-metal experimental aircraft intended for high-speed research. The pilot was lying prone in an ejectable cockpit capsule, and the aircraft was equipped with a retractable ski undercarriage.

The estimated performance of Type 346 was very good, with a ceiling of approx. 25 km, and calculated max. speed M 2. Ground and onboard instrumentation was delivered by the former Askania-Werke in Berlin. In November 1946 the first aircraft, which had been constructed in Germany, was tested in the TsAGI full-scale windtunnel T-101. As predicted, at big angles of attack there was a certain loss of longitudinal stability, as the entire wing had the same profile. The wing profile was *NACA 0,012-0,55-1,25* with a relative thickness of 12 per cent, while the radial nose cone was modelled according to *NACA 00121-0,66,50*. The area of the 45° swept wing was 19.87 m², while the all-moving stabilizer could be trimmed between –2° 40' . . . + 2°. The calculated take-off weight was 5,230-5,300 kg.

Three complete prototypes (346.1 to 346.3) and one engineless aircraft (346P) were constructed. The 346.1 was at first used as a ground-test mock-up. The available information regarding the flight testing and the status of the various prototypes is still rather ambiguous, but can be summarized as follows:

In 1948 the flying tests of the control system were started using a modified DFS Kranich sailing plane (the cockpit configuration was disliked by a number of Soviet test-pilots, among others Mark L. Gallaj).

In 1948-49 the first engineless prototype 346P (or DFS 301 — according to other information the designation of this aircraft was 346A or 346-I) was tested towed by a Junkers Ju 388 (24 flights). The take-off weight of this glider was 1,880-2,180 kg. This aircraft was later dropped from under-wing of the Boeing

B-29 Superfortress (!) 42-6358, which had made a forced landing in Siberia after bombing Japan. A total of four flights were made in this manner (compare the American launching method of the Bell X-1!). Thus approximately 30 powerless flights had been made by the 41-year old test-pilot Wolfgang Ziese at Tyeplyi Stan (in the vicinity of Moscow).

On 5 May 1949 the assembly of the first powered aircraft, the 346D (or 346-II) was completed (the rocket-engine was however only "cold", not yet in running condition). The take-off weight of this prototype was 3,145 kg. The preparation of the first flight of the 346D took all summer, and only on 30 September 1949 was the first flight made.

Ziese ejected the 346D from the host B-29 at an altitude of 9,700 m. During the flight Ziese faced a number of control problems, which had already appeared during the testing of the 346A (although not strongly enough to have raised appropriate attention).

He was however able to gain control of the aircraft, but miscalculated the landing at the high speed (310 km/h) and the 346D made a very hard landing and the ejectable landing ski was damaged. Ziese lost his conscience briefly, but was able to continue the testing of the 346 after some time in hospital.

The accident commission led by the Soviet test-pilot N.S. Rybko (HSU 1.5.1957) considered that the landing damage was caused by Ziese's handling faults — not paying due attention to the enormous difficulties he had in saving the aircraft at all!

After Ziese's hard landing, the 346D was repaired and transferred to LII, where it was flown by the Soviet test-pilot Petr I. Kaz'min. On his first unpowered flight he faced the same problems with the landing ski as Ziese had encountered, but as his flight was made in wintertime, the soft snow saved the aircraft from serious damage. Kaz'min made his second flight being towed by a Tu-2, and ejecting at an altitude of 2,000 m. The aircraft was also damaged at this landing, but his flights had however proved that the control characteristics of the 346D were now ripe for powered flight.

After the 346D had been repaired, the rocket engine was tested on the ground. The testing of the 346 was now relocated to Dukhovishchi, where the testing commenced on 12 October 1950. At Dukhovishchi Ziese performed 12 flights in the 346P being towed by a Ju 388, two flights being dropped from the B-29. Only one unsuccessful flight was made with 346.1, before the 346.3 was tested with engine power in September 1951. Being the most experienced 346-pilot, Ziese was chosen to perform the first powered flight. The host B-29 climbed to 10,000 m, where Ziese ejected and fired the rocket engines.

He soon reached a speed of 1100 km/h, but was forced to land because of vibrations in the aircraft. He was awarded a special premium of 20,000 roubles for the first powered 346-flight. After Ziese's flight two Russian test-pilots tried to repeat his performance, but problems encountered during the ejection phase from the host aircraft caused both pilots to crash with the B-29 after ejection. Both prototypes were destroyed, and one of the Russian test-pilots was killed (the other escaped by parachute). On 14 September 1951 Ziese finally encountered a break-up of the wing of 346.3 at an altitude of 20,000 m, but he was able to escape in the ejectable pressurized cockpit capsule, and landed safely by parachute.

After this loss of all three powered *Type 346* prototypes the further development of the project was transferred to the Ural area, and completely taken over by the Russians. Here the development of another DFS 346 derivative, the *Type 446*, powered by two BMW 003 jet turbines also took place.

Ziese reportedly died of cancer a few years later in a Soviet hospital.

Type 468 was a rocket-powered development of *Type 346*, the construction of which was not finished.

It is an interesting, but virtually unknown fact that simultaneously with the development of *Type 346* another experimental rocket aircraft of similar configuration, but of entirely Soviet design, was tested in the USSR! This aircraft, *Type 5*, was an all-metal aircraft designed by M.R. Bisnovat. The wing sweep was 45°, with a *TsAGI 12045bis* profile at the root and *P2(2M)* at the wing tip. Like the *Type 346* the *Type 5* was developed during 1945-48, and flight tested at LII from 1948 to 1951 in complete secrecy from the German "346-team"! The *Type 5* was powered by an RD-2M3VF rocket engine with 2,000 kp thrust, designed by L.S. Dushkin (this engine was also used in the Mikoyan I-270(Zh) experimental rocket fighter).

The *Type 5* had an estimated max. speed of M 1.13 at an altitude of 12,000-13,000 m. In the TsAGI windtunnel T-104 it had been satisfactorily tested up to M 1.45. The *Type 5* was flight tested in the same manner as the *Type 346,* ie lifted to 7,000-7,500 m altitude by a host aircraft, in this case the Petlyakov Pe-8 four-engine heavy bomber. Two prototypes, *"5-1"* and *"5-2"* were constructed.

The first flight of the first prototype *"5-1"* was performed by A.K. Pakhonov (HSU 14.1.1952) on 14 July 1948. He had difficulties in ejecting from the host aircraft and crashed into the Pe-8 but was able to make a successful forced-landing, the aircraft was however badly damaged. After repair two more flights with *"5-1"* were performed. During the third flight of *"5-1"* on 5 September 1948, the aircraft crashed beyond repair, but the pilot escaped without injury.

The second modified prototype *"5-2"* was ready for testing in January 1949. The first test flight was piloted by Georgij M. Shiyanov (HSU 1.5.57 for the testing of Sukhoi-jet prototypes), who also made a hard landing on 26 January 1949, having difficulties in estimating the landing at the relatively small landing strip of LII.

The entire programme was cancelled after Shiyanov's sixth flight of the *"5-2"* in June 1949, when a speed of M 0.775 had been reached.

An interesting reference to *Type 346* can be found in the collection of biographies of aircraft designers *Sovetskiye aviatsionnyye konstruktory* written by A.N. Ponomaryev in 1977. (Eng Col-Gen. Ponomarev had studied aircraft engine design at the National Aeronautical Institute and Sorbonne University in Paris from 1933, preparing his Doctor's dissertation in 1938. He was however ordered to return to the USSR before he was able to defend his dissertation. In

August 1939, being fluent in French, he was ordered to serve as an interpreter at the aborted tripartite military negotiations between the USSR, England and France in Moscow, literally at the eve of the signing of the Molotov-Ribbentrop pact. He was later the Director of the Air Force Academy in Leningrad, and the Chairman of the Aviation-technical Committee and a member of the Military Council of the Soviet Air Force.)

"The further creative work of . . . one of the talented Soviet designers Aleksandr Yakovlevich Bereznyak was directed towards design of liquid-fuel rocket-powered aircraft. One of the aircraft was created on **suggestion by a group of designers headed by him**. . ." (emphasis here).

According to Col-Gen (Eng) A.N. Ponomarev this "anonymous" aircraft (no identification whatsoever of the aircraft type is given, but the text is illustrated by an — for Soviet publications — unusually clear picture of Type 346 sitting on the extracted ski!) was dropped from the Tupolev Tu-4 at an altitude of 8-12 km and a speed of M 0.8, first without engine power. After the first series of powerless flights a second series of powered flights were performed at M 1.0 speed until maximum altitude was reached. Take-off weight of the aircraft was 5,230 kg, wings swept 45 degrees. The tests were cancelled in 1951 after an accident which forced the pilot to catapult.

However, this extremely interesting brief account of the result of "the group of designers headed by Bereznyak" is *missing* from the second and third editions of Ponomarev's book, published in 1980 and 1990 respectively (indicating that the censors made a mistake when passing the first edition for publication?).

Many of the Germans working in *OKB-1* and *OKB-2* were eventually to return to (West-)Germany and Austria in the mid-1950s when most of the German prisoners-of-war were repatriated (nb: the German engineers were not of course prisoners-of-war as they were only forced to go to the USSR in October 1946 — nearly 18 months after the German capitulation!)

After the return of the German engineers a number of accounts of the work performed in the USSR were published in various Western aviation journals. As many of these articles were — for obvious reasons — published anonymously, appropriate attention was not always paid to the — naturally rather vague — information content, which was considered either "*science fiction*" (in the literal meaning of this phrase!) or on the other hand as the *definite proof,* badly needed by the Cold War anti-Soviet propagandists that the MiG-15 etc were of German origin!

The Soviet designers obviously soon learned via Alekseyev and Bereznyak what they needed from the Germans, and applied this know-how very skilfully in their own Design Bureaux, after which the German OKBs were considered unnecessary and were closed down. The full history of the German OKBs in Russia will probably be hidden forever in inaccessible Russian archives.

The development of the DFS 346 experimental supersonic rocket-powered aircraft was completed in the Soviet Union after the war. It was flight-tested by Wolfgang Ziese in 1951. The first lifts to launching altitude were made by one of the Boeing B-29s which had landed in Siberia in 1945. These pictures seem however to depict the Soviet-built copy Tupolev Tu-4 (c/n 230503) as mother aircraft. Note the attachment of the DFS 346 under the wings between the engines.

A poor quality — but extremely rare photograph of a Junkers Ju 388 with red stars. The Ju 388 was used in 1948-50 for the first towing experiments of the DFS-346 experimental supersonic aircraft in the Soviet Union.

The Baade 150 jet bomber prototype. The "bicycle type" undercarriage with auxiliary support wheels at the wingtips, the extremely forward-swept underwing engine pylons and distinct overwing air layer fences are noteworthy.

Extract from *Sovietskiye aviatsionniye konstruktory* by A.N. Ponomaryev (1977) with caption "Experimental flying laboratory" — ie. the DFS 346, the identity of which was not revealed at that time!

An intriguing piece of German war booty (?) in the Soviet Air Force Museum at Monino in 1984: note the inscription ". . .boten" on the back wall behind the MiG-25 — the obvious obliteration of the beginning of the text "Rauchen verboten" can be recognized. Was this hangar (or part of its structure) transported from Germany after the war — or did it house German specialists — or aircraft — at some time? (Unfortunately the author only detected this inscription when inspecting his photographs at home after his visit to Monino, and thus had no opportunity of asking for an explanation.)

APPENDIX 1

Early German influence on Soviet aviation

In 1921 the Soviet government decided to buy aircraft and aero-engines from abroad, with the objective of creating an indigenous high-level aviation industry by studying the best aircraft types available on the world market. In longer view the aim was to establish a highly potent air force, equipped primarily with Soviet-designed and produced aircraft.

In spite of the difficult economic situation the considerable sum of three million gold roubles was allocated by the Soviet government for the purpose of purchasing pattern aircraft, aero-engines and production technology. Contacts were made to all major aircraft producing countries, but because of the political situation the "German connection" was to have a special significance.

During the NEP period there were favourable political relations with Germany since the signing of the so-called Treaty of Rapallo between Soviet Russia and Germany (named after the small north Italian town where the treaty was signed on 16 April 1922). The Treaty was the first *de jure* international recognition of the Soviet government, and led to the establishment of diplomatic relations, economic and commercial co-operation.

During this first "honeymoon" German companies were granted concessions and invited to create joint enterprises in the Soviet Union, operating in the service trade as well as in the industrial sectors. The best known German-Russian companies of this period were:

DERULUFT air transport company, or *Deutsch-Russische Luftverkehrs-Gesellschaft* (with the main route Königsberg, later Berlin — Moscow with the Fokker F.III, Junkers F.13 and ANT-9 aircraft), and

DERUTA shipping company handling sea transports in the Baltic Sea.

Lesser known were DERUMETALL (scrap metal trading company) and RUSSGERTORG (general trading).

A special significance was given to the manufacture of military equipment and arms in Soviet Russia based on German licences and technology. As all military production in Germany was prohibited by the Versailles Treaty, both the German government and the German industry were interested in utilizing and updating the German military know-how. On the other hand, the Soviets had a pressing desire to reconstruct their industry, devastated by the revolution and civil war, and as they were not a party to the Treaty of Versailles they had no formal reason to prevent German rearmament. The access to modern armament technology offered by the Germans was certainly not unattractive.

In Germany the cover organisation *Gesellschaft zur Förderung Gewerblicher Unternehmen (GEFU)* (supported by the Reichswehr-ministerium), with a capital of

75 million Reichsmarks, was set up to administer military production, including: the Junkers company which founded an aircraft factory at Fili, in the vicinity of Moscow. Junkers even acquired a concession to operate airline traffic on a few internal Russian routes, and a poison gas manufacturing company named BERSOL, which started its activities in Samara, GEFU also supervised the manufacture of artillery ammunition at factories in Tula, Leningrad and Schlisselburg. According to one American report the Krupp company was constructing 17 (!) shell and artillery plants in 1927.

Junkers concession

Already on 6 February 1922 (ie even before the signing of the Rapallo Treaty) a preliminary agreement was signed with Junkers according to which the former *Russo-Baltijskiy Vagonny Zavod (RVBZ)* at Fili was handed over to the Junkers company, which correspondingly would start the production of all-metal aircraft there.

The Junkers investment included a guarantee capital of approx. 600 million Reichsmarks, construction materials, metal cutting machines and special tools (to the value of 150 million RM), drawings and documentation (150 million RM), and technical and commercial experience and expertise, including factory management (100 million RM). The Junkers investment totalled approx. 1,100 million RM. The German government granted up to 140 million RM to Junkers, a secret agreement between the *Reichswehrministerium* and Junkers being signed on 15 March 1922.

On 29 January 1923 Junkers was officially granted a concession by the Soviet government. Operations at Fili started rapidly, the number of Russian and German employees rising to over 1,350. From 1923 to 1926 a total of some 170 aircraft were manufactured, including 122 Ju 21 fighters (German designations T21 and H21), 40 Ju 20 reconnaissance aircraft (German designation A 20), and Ju 13 passenger aircraft (German designation F.13). A few aircraft were assembled at Fili from parts imported from Germany, in addition to approx. 50 Junkers F.13s delivered from the Junkers parent company at Dessau.

A number of BMW IIIa engines were also assembled at Fili – later to be manufactured as M-17 in the Soviet Union.

On 1 March 1927 the Junkers concession was unexpectedly cancelled. The formal reasons for the cancellation of the concession were an alleged breach of the contractual obligations from the Junkers side, as no construction of an aero-engine factory was undertaken, and the promised transfer of duraluminium technology and know-how to the Soviet industry had not taken place.

On the other hand, according to the generally accepted German view of the situation the Fili company was practically bankrupt in 1926, because of the hyper-inflation in Germany, no possibility of profit transfers to the Junkers parent company in Germany, and continual problems with the Soviet labour legislations and raw material supplies. The only real compensation the German government got was the delivery of 300,000 artillery shells "Made in USSR".

The Junkers parent company incurred tremendous losses, and as no operating funds were available after the cancellation of the state guarantees, there was no other possibility but to close the Fili works. A detailed memorandum was presented in the German parliament, exposing the secret economical co-operation between Germany and the Soviet Union.

However, the level of the Soviet aircraft industry was considerably raised, competent personnel were trained, modern technology, production methods and machinery were acquired. The East German history of the Junkers company (published in 1986) has summarized the Soviet gains in a nutshell: ". . . (it) enabled the Soviet aircraft industry to develop its own modern aircraft designs and in a comparable short time to produce its own efficient aircraft." The Soviet part had thus achieved all its original aims and cancelled the Junkers concession as soon as the know-how potential available had been transferred to the Soviet specialists working at Fili.

Tupolev's first all-metal aircraft were certainly very much influenced by technology transferred during the Junkers' Soviet venture, which is witnessed by the fact that production of the TB-1 (or ANT-4) bomber was undertaken at Fili after closing down of the Junkers concession in late 1926. Junkers even tried — without success — to take Tupolev and TsAGI to court for breach of Junkers' patents concerning certain features of all-metal wing structures.

Lipetsk flying school

In parallel with the industrial and economic co-operation referred to above there were also clandestine direct military contacts between the two countries, as the German army was granted the possibility of establishing a number of secret training facilities on the territory of the Soviet Union.

In 1923 a series of negotiations between the *Reichswehr* and the Red Army commenced, leading to the setting up of a number of special military-technical schools for the training of German specialists: a military flying school at Lipetsk (north of Voronezh), a gas warfare school in Saratov and a tank school in Kazan. An exchange of military delegations observing manoeuvres in the two countries was organized, special naval equipment was delivered from Germany, and even the design for the "S" or "Stalinets" class of long-range patrol submarines was ordered from the German-financed submarine design-bureau *Ingenieurskantoor voor Scheepsbouw* (*I.v.S.*) at The Hague, in the Netherlands.

As the history of the Lipetsk flying school has been told elsewhere (*see* Lennart Andersson's article in Air International No 41/summer 1990), it will be only briefly summarized here.

A German liaison office, the *Sondergruppe Moskau* (completely separated from the German embassy in Moscow) led by *Oberst* Lieth-Thomsen had been set up to keep contact with the Soviet authorities. On 15 April 1925 an agreement was signed concerning the establishing of a flying school (under the cover name *Wissenschaftliche Versuchs- und Prüfunganstalt für Luftfahrzeuge — Wipuwal*) at Lipetsk. Flying training began in the summer of 1925 and continued until 1933 when the facility was closed down, as both the German and the Soviet partners had lost interest in further activities. The German funding of the rather expensive Lipetsk operation was also very difficult, and it had to be carefully disguised for secrecy reasons. As at this time military aviation training could already be more or less openly (and cheaper! — which was a very important argument during the depression) organized in Germany, it was decided to close down the Lipetsk school. The Soviets had nothing against closing the school and getting rid of the Germans as there was no more information to be gained for the Soviet benefit (the aircraft used at Lipetsk were already considered obsolete), and they were, on the contrary, becoming suspicious of the considerable number of German officers on their territory (the German flying school shared the Lipetsk air base with a Soviet AF unit!).

A total of some 120 fighter pilots (of which many were First World War veterans) and also some ex-civilian pilots, as well as a similar number of observers had been trained at Lipetsk. The main aircraft types used at Lipetsk were the Fokker D.XIII fighters, 50 of which were ordered from Holland in 1925. Later a number of Heinkel HD 17 reconnaissance and Junkers light bombers were also delivered. The aircraft were usually flown to the USSR along the normal Deruluft route from Königsberg, except the first batch of Fokker D.XIIIs which were delivered by ship to Leningrad. When the Lipetsk school was

A line-up of Heinkel HD 17 aircraft (5 recce and 2 trainer aircraft) at Lipetsk.

Approximately 50 Fokker D.XIII fighters were used at the clandestine German Military Flying School at Lipetsk. When the German activities were closed down, the remaining 30 fighters were handed over to the Soviets. The depicted "11" is c/n 4613.

closed down in September 1933 the Germans took all the aircraft with them except some 30 remaining obsolete Fokker D.XIIIs, which were handed over to the Soviets.

Licence-production of Dornier and Heinkel aircraft

In addition to the Junkers concession the Soviets also had contacts with other German manufacturers, and big orders for aircraft were placed with Dornier and Heinkel in the 1920s and 1930s.

Dornier J Wal

In 1926-27, 22 Dornier J Wal flying-boats were procured to be used in the Black Sea, followed later by some ten flying-boats. The aircraft, to be delivered to the Soviet Union,

A Dornier "Wal" of the
Air Force of the Black Sea
Fleet at Sevastopol,
Crimea.

The Dornier Wal was also
used in the Arctic regions.
CCCP-H2 of
V.S. Molokov (who was
later one of the very first
HSUs after the *Chelyushkin*
rescue operation in 1934)
is greeted by an
enthusiastic public at the
Moskva river in 1936.

were built in Italy, and equipped with various engines: Lorraine-Dietrich (450 hp), or BMW VI (500 hp). In 1930 a batch was delivered without engines, as the Soviet-built M-17 (licence-produced BMW VI) were installed on delivery.

According to Shavrov six Wal flying boats were produced in Sevastopol in 1931-33, although this has not been verified.

The sturdy Dornier Wal flying-boats were primarily used in the Arctic regions.

Heinkel HD 37 (I-7)

The prototype of the Heinkel HD 37 fighter biplane powered by a BMW VI-engine was tested in the Soviet Union at the end of the 1920s. During a test flight in August 1927 the NII VVS test-pilot Viktor Osipovich Pisarenko was forced to escape by parachute at only 100 metres after the aircraft started spinning. However, the HD 37 was subsequently licence-produced in the Soviet Union as the I-7 (with the engine correspondingly changed to the Soviet-built M-17) in small numbers at the beginning of the 1930s. The production ended in 1934 in favour of the superior Polikarpov I-15.

Left and overleaf: The Heinkel HD 37 fighter was manufactured in the Soviet Union as the 1-7, and used on skis in winter-time.

Heinkel HD 55 (KR-1)

By the end of the 1920s Ernst Heinkel had gained reputation as a designer of successful maritime aircraft. Via the Soviet trade delegation in Berlin a visit of a high Soviet delegation led by the Deputy Commander of the Soviet Air Force Jakov I. Alksnis,[21] and including the TsAGI representative N.M. Kharlamov[22] and S.A. Mezheninov (Chief of Staff of the Air Force since 1923, and future Deputy Commander of VVS) to the Heinkel company on 22 January 1929. The Soviets were interested if Heinkel would be able to design a catapult (max. length 21.5 m) for an unnamed warship, and a prototype aircraft according to their technical specifications.

---

[21] 1897-1938, from 1931 Commander of the Soviet Air Force. Arrested in November 1937, executed on 29 July 1938.

[22] Director of TsAGI from 1932 until his arrest in early 1938 in connection with the Tupolev espionage accusations. He was obviously not given the same opportunity as Tupolev to work at a "*sharaga*", but disappeared from history. It may be assumed that he was sent to a Gulag camp or executed.

The Heinkel HD 55 was a two-seat maritime reconnaissance biplane aircraft powered by a 480 hp M-22 engine, derived from the Bristol Jupiter, and as the preliminary tests were successful a batch of 20 aircraft (and two catapults) were ordered six weeks later from the Heinkel company in Germany in 1930. In his memoirs Ernst Heinkel describes with some admiration the exact work of the Soviet acceptance commission, checking all details, investigating all materials against the specifications, and so on, putting a lot of extra load on his engineers. The Soviet orders however helped the company to overcome the depression.

In the Soviet Union the Heinkel HD 55 was redesignated KR-1 (*Korabelnyj razvedchik* = Shipborne recce aircraft). The KR-1 were used at least on the battleship *Parizhskaya Kommuna* (ex-*Sevastopol*) of the Black Sea fleet, and probably also the similar *Oktyabrskaya Revolutsiya* (ex-*Gangut*) and *Marat* (ex-*Petropavlovsk*) of the Baltic Fleet until 1938.

The Heinkel HD 55 (KR-1) was used by the Red Navy in the early 1930s. No "3" is being lifted aboard the battleship *Parizhskaya kommuna* of the Baltic Fleet in 1932.

A Heinkel HD 55 (KR-1) No "2" is catapult-launched.

When the world was shocked by the signing of the Ribbentrop-Molotov pact on 23 August 1939, leading to a new round of intense economic and industrial co-operation between the "incompatible allies", there were thus old traditions and personal contacts to utilize — as three of the major German aircraft manufacturers (Junkers, Heinkel and Dornier) had been directly (albeit clandestinely) involved in Soviet projects a mere decade earlier.

In retrospect it is rather strange that the cover-up of the many-faceted pre-war Soviet-German military co-operation remained so tight until long after the Second World War.

Aircraft based at Lipetsk 1925-1933
(courtesy of Lennart Andersson)

Type	Qty	Period of service	Known identities
Fokker D.XIII	50	1925-33	1 to 50/ (D2252)
Junkers A 20	2	1925-31	(D750)
Albatros L 69	2	1925-27	
Fokker D.VII	2	1926-33	
Junkers F.13	1	1926-33	(D252)
Heinkel HD 21	1	1926-30*	
Heinkel HD 17	7	1926-33	I, II, III, IV, V, "G"
Albatros L 76a	6 (1)	1927-31	1 to 6
Heinkel HD 40 II	1	1928-33	(D1180)
Albatros L 77v	6	1928	(D1546 to 1549, 1573, 1574)
Albatros L 78	6 (2)	1929-33	(D2093, 2094, 2098, 2099, 2467, 2487)
Dornier B Merkur	1	1929-31	(D970)
Rohrbach Ro VIII	1 (3)	1929-32*	97/ (D991)
Junkers W 33b	1	1930-33	(D1534)
Junkers A 48 (K 47)	3	1930-33	"J/(D1057)
Junkers W 34fi (K 43)	2	1930-33*	"K"/(D1844, 1845)
BFW M 23c	1	1931-33	(D1884)

* not confirmed
(1) In addition, D1127 was used for tests
(2) In addition, D1524 was used for tests
(3) Used for tests in 1928 and 1929
Notes: The table does not include aircraft used at Lipetsk for testing only.

Above and below: The Ju 20 was manufactured at Fili and used extensively by the Red Navy.
The Finnish-born Otto A. Kalvits used a Ju 20 for a flight to Novaya Zemlya in 1925.

APPENDIX 2

Baltic AF units in Luftwaffe and VVS

2.1 From Sonderstaffel Buschmann to NSGr 11

The Estonian Air Force had acquired at least five Henschel Hs 126Bs in the autumn of 1939. After the Sovietization of Estonia in summer 1940, what was left of the former Estonian army was reorganized as the 22nd Territorial Corps of the Red Army. A large number of the military personnel of the former Estonian armed forces had however been arrested by the Soviet security organs of the infamous NKVD and deported to Siberia. These "bourgois" elements were — at least — partly replaced with Estonian communists who had emigrated to Soviet Russia after the Estonian Liberation War 1919, and now returned in order to assist in the Sovietization of their native country. The remnants of the Estonian Air Force were transformed into the Aircraft Squadron of the 22nd Corps, with Jägala as its main base, flying their remaining serviceable aircraft marked with "red stars". After the German attack on the Soviet Union on 22 June 1941, the 22nd Squadron was ordered to retreat to Russia on 27 June with its few serviceable aircraft, the most potent being a handful of Avro Ansons and Hs 126s. A number of aircraft are reported to have been flown to Russia, and all others were burned and destroyed. The national Estonian unit of the VVS had thus virtually ceased to exist.

Meanwhile many of the Estonian pilots had taken to the woods in order to await the advancing Germans and join the *Metsavennad* ("Brethren of the Forest") freedom fighters. However, the Soviet Baltic fleet apparently found three Henschels which had escaped destruction, from which the aircraft used by Maj. Koronets (CO of 71 IAP) in July-August 1941 was chosen (see section on the Henschel Hs 126 for details).

Luftwaffe was also to incorporate a national Estonian unit. First set up more or less as a "private venture", and known as the volunteer *Sonderstaffel Buschmann*, it was organized by the enigmatic Balt-German Gerhard Buschmann, who had been Flying Instructor of the Estonian Aero Club (and simultaneously the *Abwehr* representative in Tallinn!).

One of the Estonian sailplane pilots trained by Buschmann, Harald Mang, witnessed the attacks and shooting down by two Soviet SB-2 bombers (of 1 MTAP of the Air Force of the Baltic Fleet) of the Finnish Junkers Ju 52 airliner OH-ALL *Kaleva* en route from Tallinn to Helsinki on 14 June 1940. The reason for this blatant attack on a civil airliner of a neutral country has never been explained (the peace agreement between Finland and the Soviet Union ending the Winter War had been signed on 13 March 1940), but was obviously connected with the forthcoming Sovietization of Estonia. The shooting down of *Kaleva* with

An ex-Estonian Henschel Hs 126B of the Aviation Squadron of the 22nd Territorial Corps of the Red Army at Jägala, Estonia in March 1941. The Estonian tricolor triangular national insignia have been overpainted with red stars. The airmen are all Estonians (from left to right): Remi Milk (later served in 3./SAGr 127 and escaped to Sweden in an Arado Ar 95 on 21 September 1944), Tarmo Rae and Vello Maks (KIA during the war).

all on board killed (a crew of two and seven passengers, including American, German and French diplomatic couriers) was for many years more or less a "taboo" of the sensitive Finnish-Soviet relations after the Second World War. Buschmann however told the Finnish accident investigation commission in July 1941 about the observations of his pupil Mang, who happened to perform his military service as an observer in the Keri lighthouse at the time of the shooting down of the *Kaleva*. The report of Mang as retold by Buschmann, and printed in a document collection, the *Finnish Blue-White Book Vol. 2* (published by the Finnish Foreign Ministry in 1941), was basically confirmed in the memoirs of Lt-Gen. Pyotr I. Khokhlov in 1988. Khokhlov, who was to end his career as Chief of Staff of the Air Forces of the Soviet Navy had served as navigator in one of the aircraft attacking *Kaleva*.

"*Sonderstaffel Buschmann*" was formed on 12 February 1942 at Ülemiste, and had a very peculiar organization: it was part of *Kriegsmarine*, but depended on *Luftflotte 1* regarding supply and technical support, and its salaries were furthermore paid by the SS (as a "special police unit" — which gives a hint of some of the tasks the unit performed!). The Sonderstaffel (identification code SB + __) flew its first missions patrolling the Gulf of Finland with various secondhand aircraft including four Estonian PTO-4 light aircraft (designed by the Estonian engineers Post, Tooma and Org) in March 1942, coded SB + AA, + AB to + AD. In May-June 1942 more aircraft were acquired: a Miles Magister (coded SB+ AF), a RWD-8 (coded SB + AJ), a DH-89A Dragon Rapide (which had belonged to the Latvian state-owned airline Valts Gaisa Satiksme, coded SB + AH), four Stampe SV-5 light aircraft (the Latvian VEF factory had produced ten SV-5s under a Belgian licence, one code known: SB + AK). The personnel used uniforms of the old Estonian Air Force (or civil dresses) with Estonian emblems, and although the aircraft carried normal German insignia (*Balken-* and *Hakenkreuz*) the propeller spinners were painted in the Estonian colours blue-black-white.

In summer 1942 28 Heinkel He 60s and a number of Arado Ar 95s were acquired.

A number of Fokker C.VEs were captured by Soviet forces in autumn 1944 in the Baltic area. These aircraft had a very complicated history: originally delivered to the Danish Air Force, they were taken over by the Luftwaffe after the German occupation of Denmark in 1940, and subsequently equipped the NAGr 11 (ex-SAGr 127) which was formed of Estonian volunteers. The 3W + OS seems to be in intact condition, while the other two aircraft are certain not to fly again. *Note*: In October 1944 two Fokker C.VEs of NSGr 11 were flown by their Estonian crews to Sweden from Latvia and East Prussia respectively.

The Sonderstaffel also underwent a number of organizational changes: in July 1942 it was reformed as 15./AGr 127, which was expanded to full *Gruppe* (AGr 127) in April 1943, consisting of Stab, and three Staffeln: 1(F). — long-range maritime recce squadron, 2(*M and Stör*). — short-range maritime recce and light attack squadron, 3(*Ausb.* and *Verb.*) — training and liaison squadron. In mid-1943 the *Gruppe* incorporated 40-50 aircraft, and flew primarily from Ülemiste, Rahkala and Jōhvi. The Ar 95 seaplanes of 1./AGr 127 operated from Ülemiste, and the other two *Staffeln* used various frontline bases for nocturnal bombing.

On 18 October 1943 the AGr 127 was split up into two main units: the former maritime *1. Staffel* becoming SAGr 127 (using Ar 95s from Ülemiste; unit code 6R +), while the other two *Staffeln* formed the new NSGr 11 using land-based Heinkel He 50 aircraft. On 27 December 1943 a third *Staffel* was added to NSGr 11 at Johvi with Arado Ar 66s (unit code 3W +). In February-March 1944 NSGr 11 got more aircraft: twenty ex-Danish Fokker CVEs captured by *Luftwaffe*. In 1944 NSGr 11 operated primarily in Kurland subordinated to *Fliegerdivision* 3 (with bases at Jōhvi, Rahkla, Reval/Tallinn and Libau/Liepaja).

In September 1944 the NSGr 11 was based at Poltsamaa near Tallinn, and was transferred to Libau with seven Fokker CVEs, seventeen He 50s and thirteen Ar 66s.

After the Soviet occupation of Estonia in late September 1944, the motivation of the Estonian units to continue fighting on the German side diminished and a number of aviators tried to escape to Sweden: on 22 September three Ar 95s (6R + LL, 6R + BL, 6R + UL) of 3./SAGr 127, on 1 October one Fokker CVEs (3W + OL) and one Heinkel He 50 (3W + NO) of NSGr 11, and finally the Fokker CVE (3W + OD) flew to Sweden. The Estonian NSGr 11 was finally dissolved as unreliable by *Luftflotte* 1 at Libau-Nord on 4 October 1944.

Estonians in the Soviet Air Force
A number of Estonian aviators also served in the Soviet Air Force. These Estonians were mostly determined communists who had already emigrated to the Soviet Union after the Estonian Liberation War in 1919, or who in some cases had been evacuated to the Soviet Union after the German attack in 1941. At least the following Estonian aviators commanded aviation regiments of the Soviet Air Force:

Endel K. Pusep (1909-), who had served as a polar aviator taking part in several Arctic expeditions at the end of the 1930s. On 11-12 August 1941 he took part in the famous Berlin attack with Pe-8 heavy bombers of 81 AD taking off from Pushkino near Leningrad, making a forced landing on the return leg. Between 19 May and 13 June 1942 he flew the Soviet Foreign Minister V.M. Molotov in a Pe-8 from Moscow to Dundee and Washington, D.C. for meetings with the Allied leaders, for which Pusep was awarded the HSU on 20 June 1942. In October 1942 he was appointed CO of the Pe-8 equipped 890 AP of ADD. After the war he served for some years as Social Minister of the Estonian SSR.

Aleksandr Jakobson was CO of 99 BBAP from January 1943. This unit was later 96 GvBAP, and bombed the Reichstag building in the German capital in May 1945 for which it was awarded the "*Berlinskij*" honorary title.

Karl Kerro was CO of the famous 159 IAP of 275 IAD from March 1945.

Leonid Rejno was CO of 215 ShAP in 1941, and later headed the Department of Shturmovik Training at the Soviet Air Force HQ.

Eduard Vijk served in autumn 1944 as CO of 6 (Polish) ShAP "*Brandenburgskij*", which belonged to the 2 Polish Aviation Corps of the Soviet Air Force.

The closest to an Estonian national unit in the Soviet Air Force was the "*Tasuja*" (Avenger) detached night bombing squadron (87 ONBAE) using Polikarpov Po-2 light aircraft. This squadron which belonged to the 13th Air Army was formed on funds collected among Estonians in the Soviet Union. CO was the Russian Maj. Dmitrij Telegin, while the Chief of Staff from 15 September 1944 was the Estonian Ivan Tambaum. The composition of the personnel was "international", ie probably mostly Russian as in most other units of the Soviet Air Force. In autumn 1944 the "*Tasuja*" squadron operated in the Baltic area, bombing among others Johvi and Kuremäe — ie the NSG 11 operating area.

2.2 Latvian airmen in Luftwaffe and VVS

As in Estonia the former Latvian Army was transferred into the 24th Territorial Corps of the Red Army commanded by Lt.-Gen. P.J. Klyavinsh, with the Latvian Army Air Force correspondingly transferred into the Detached Aviation Squadron of the 24th Corps. This squadron, with a personnel of 197 men and equipped with obsolete Belgian two-seater Stampe SV-5 aircraft (speed only 250 km/h), performed recce flights from their base at Gulbene during the first days after the German attack. On 27 June 1941 the *escadrille* was given a suicidal task to intercept German bombers attacking Aluksne with three SV-5s. One of the three aircraft was shot down with the pilot Sn-Ltn Greizis killed while the navigator Sn-Ltn Briedis escaped by parachute. During the night between 28 and 29 June all remaining aircraft were given the order to fly east via Irditsa and Velikiye Luki to Rhzev, where the aircraft and eight aviators arrived on 2 July. In Rzhev the few aircraft were deemed not airworthy, and the aviators were ordered to continue to Moscow by train and report in the Main Administration of the Soviet Air Force. The train to Moscow was however bombed by German aircraft, and some Latvian pilots were killed or injured. Thus the Latvian Detached Aviation Squadron had practically ceased to exist and the remaining personnel were organized into a Latvian reserve regiment (the main part of the personnel had meanwhile travelled by trucks from Gulbene to Torzhok).

On 20 January 1943 the General Staff of the Red Army however gave permission to reorganize the Latvian Aviation Squadron. The Latvian VVS personnel had meanwhile been collected into 6 ZABr (Reserve Aviation Brigade) in Tula, and on 15 March 1943 the newly-formed squadron with Polikarpov Po-2 biplanes was born. To this *escadrille* arrived not only personnel of the former 24th Latvian Aviation Squadron, but also civilian Soviet pilots of Latvian nationality, Latvian youngsters who had acquired elementary flight training in avaiation clubs etc. and also Latvian airmen serving in other VVS regiments. The newly-formed squadron was subsequently transformed into a regiment, the 1st Latvian NBAP commanded by Maj. Kārlis A. Kirss (subordinated to 242 NBAD and 6th Air Army). In January 1944 the Latvian regiment was subordinated to 313 NBAD of 15th Air Army. In July it was awarded the honorary title "*Rezhitskij*" for its participation in the liberalization of Rezekne. In April 1945 it was finally subordinated to 284 NBAD. The 1st Latvian NBAP performed a total of 6450 missions, dropped 1000 tons of bombs, destroyed approx. 40 enemy aircraft, 100 guns and over 500 trucks.

Except the well-known French volunteer "*Normandie-Niemen*" regiment the 1st Latvian NBAP was the only national regiment of the VVS.

Note: There was also another VVS unit with special relations to Latvia: the "*Latvijskij strelok*" (Latvian sharpshooter) squadron consisting of ten Yakovlev Yak-7Bs acquired for 4 million roubles collected among Latvians in the Soviet Union. The aircraft were handed over in February 1943 to the squadron CO HSU Nikolaj G. Pinchuk (HSU 19.4.1945, scoring a total of 18 kills) and bore the inscription in Latvian ("*Latviesu strélneks*" and Russian. The honorary name "Latvian sharpshooter" refers to the Latvian guard unit which was one of the best organized units of the Red Army in the Russian civil war 1918-19. The squadron belonged to the 18 Guards IAP "*Vitebskij*" (ex 6 IAP, commanded by Lt-Col A.Ye. Golubov, HSU 29.6.1945 with a total of 14 kills) which fought along with the French *Normandie-Niemen* regiment as part of 303 IAD (commanded by Gen. Georgi

M. Zakharov). The "Latvian" squadron performed over 300 missions, and scored 52 air victories for two own losses before the Yak-7 aircraft were replaced with newer Yaks.

A line-up of Yak-7Bs of the "*Latviesu strélnieks*" (Latvian sharpshooter) escadrille of 18 Guards IAP in February 1943. According to *Pravda* of 21 July 1943, the escadrille had scored 12 victories without own losses.

Practically simultaneously, in September 1943 Luftflotte 1 decided to organize an aviation school for Estonian and Latvian volunteers named "*Ergänzungs-Nachtschlachtgruppe Ostland*" (ENO; commanded by the German Maj. Endress with an Estonian and a Latvian liaison officer) at Liepaja (based on the "*Flugzeugführerschule A/B Libau-Grobin*"). The ENO-volunteers were recruited from former Latvian aviators, the Latvian homeguard "*Aizsargi*" and members of the Latvian Aero Club. The ENO was equipped with Bücker Bü 131 Jungmanns, Arado Ar 66s and Gotha Go 45s training aircraft.

In March 1944 the 1st Latvian air squadron "*Nachtschlachtstaffel 1*" (commanded by *Hauptmann* Salmins) was organized with 18 Arado Ar 66 aircraft at Libau. In April 1944 the squadron was based in Veumi and assigned to NSGr 3 of *Fliegerdivision 3* and operated in the Courland area. On 23 May 1944 the aviation school at Libau/Grobin was divided into two parts, the Estonians leaving for Pärnu and the Latvians remaining. In June 1944 a second squadron (commanded by *Hauptmann Capt* Augusts Graudins) was organized at Schwanenburg, and the two squadrons formed *Nachtschlachtgruppe 12* (commanded by the German *Hauptmann* Rademacher, and from 18 August 1944 *Oberstleutnant* Nikolais Bulmanis). The unit code of NSGr 12 was 6A + . A third (fighter) squadron (commanded by *Hauptmann* Greizis) was formed in July 1944 at Riga-Spilve, but it was disbanded after a few weeks because of lack of aircraft. A planned assignment of Junkers Ju 87 Stukas also had to be cancelled because of lack of aircraft. The hardest day of fighting of the Latvian unit was 23 July 1944 when only nine aircraft out of sixteen of *2. Staffel* returned. On 11 August 1944 NSGr 12 was reorganized as *Luftwaffen Legion Lettland* commanded by *Oberstleutnant* Janis Rucels, consisting of the training school *ENG-Lettland* at Liepaja/Grobin, NSGr 12 with 3 squadrons, one fighter squadron to be formed, and one anti-aircraft artillery battalion.

After the heavy summer campaign in 1944 NSGr 12 was finally dissolved on 8 October 1944 at Serocki, Bromberg as the German command no longer considered it trustworthy after the loss of the Baltic area, and a number of defections to neutral Sweden.

From March 1944 to 1 October 1944 the *1. Staffel* had performed approx. 3500 missions and the *2. Staffel* 2658 missions, main operating areas being Pskov, Ostrov, Opochka, Gulbone, Riga, Siauliau and Peipus.

An OKL order requesting urgent formation of Estonian and Latvian *fighter units* was issued on 31 May 1944. Only two weeks later, five Latvian pilots selected from 1./NSGr 12 were posted to the Stralsund fighter-training school in Germany. After completing their retraining on the Fw 190A, all five Latvian pilots were detailed to join the famous JG 54 '*Grünherz*' in Courland, Latvia.

In fact, it is now known that due to the heavy losses in the West the OKL had intended to gradually replace most of the German pilots of JG 54 with Estonian and Latvian pilots, but this notion was dropped following the military reverses in the Baltic and the defections of several Estonian and Latvian pilots to Sweden in October 1944.

As a result, all five Latvian Fw 190 pilots were withdrawn from JG 54 and grounded, together with another six Latvian pilots still at the fighter-training school. However, after the personal intervention of their former commander, Major Endres, the OKL relented and all five qualified Latvian Fw 190 pilots were detailed to JG 1 'Oesau'. In subsequent actions, all five Latvian fighter pilots were shot down during unequal encounters over Germany, but only one was killed in action.

Fw Harijs Klints of 1./JG 1 lost his life together with his commander, Hptm Georg Hackbarth, on 1 January 1945, during the ill-starred '*Operation Bodenplatte*' — low-level surprise strike on Allied airfields. While attacking St. Denis-Westrem near Gent in Belgium, both Fw 190s were intercepted and shot down by Polish-flown Spitfires. In the case of Fw Klints it was an ironic tragedy: his victor, Warrant Officer Stanislaw Bednarczyk of 308 Sqn, RAF, was a man from his neighbouring country and, like the victim, far from his native land, in a strange uniform over a strange land.

(Incidentally, this last flight of Fw Klints formed a chapter in the German book *Start im Morgengrauen* . . . (Flight into Oblivion) about Luftwaffe fighter pilots missing in action. Fw Klints' fate was not cleared up until 1967, when this editor managed to contact witnesses and establish the last resting place of this missing pilot.)

Another group of five Latvian pilots was sent to Germany for training in July 1944, and were subsequently assigned EJG 1 in November 1944, and finally to JG 4 at Jüterbock near Berlin in March 1945 when only three Latvian pilots remained. Due to shortage of fuel and aircraft they were able to perform only a few combat missions.

2.3 The end of Lithuanian AF in 1941

The fate of the air force of the third Baltic country, Lithuania, in WW II is similar to that of Estonia and Latvia, but differs naturally in details.

When Lithuania was Sovietized on 3 August 1940, the Lithuanian army formed the 29th Territorial Corps of the Red Army. Many of the former military personnel were naturally enough "not co-operative" — many had already left the country, or would be deported to the Gulag camps. The CO of the former Lithuanian air force, Gen. Anastas Gustaitis was arrested by Soviet forces when he tried to escape to Germany on 22 June 1941, and was subsequently executed in Moscow on 16 October 1941.

The air force, the *Karo Aviacija* was similarly transformed into the Eskadrilya of the 29th Corps (also called the *Tautine Eskadrile,* or national squadron). The squadron which was commanded by Maj. Ju. Kovas possessed 23 aircraft: nine Anbo-41 recce aircraft, one

Gloster Gladiator I, three Bücker Bü 133 Jungmeisters, three Anbo-51 trainers and some Anbo-4 recce aircraft.

On 22 June 1941 the squadron was located near Ukmere in the Divonya forest with 13 serviceable aircraft: nine Anbo-41s, the Gladiator I fighter and three Anbo-51 trainers. The next day Maj. Kovas ordered the servicable aircraft to fly eastwards to Pabrad, but many aviators disobeyed the order and flew in the other direction instead, landing their aircraft in front of the advancing German forces.

During the retreat Jun-Lt A. Morkus was accidentally killed in the Gladiator, while the Anbo of the squadron CO Maj. Kovas was shot down by Soviet PVO in Belorussia.

In 1943, 1.5 million roubles were collected among Lithuanians evacuated to the Soviet mainland for construction of a Yak-7 equipped fighter escadrille named *"Tarybu Lietuvà"* (Soviet Lithuania) for the Soviet Air Force.

APPENDIX 3

Heroes of the Soviet Union fighting against the VVS — ex-Luftwaffe pilots in the VVS?
A voluntary Russian aviation unit commanded by Maj. Filatov was already formed within *Heeresgruppe Mitte* in summer 1942. The large number of Soviet AF pilots voluntarily arriving on the German side with their aircraft (a total of 66 aircraft in 1943, and a further 20 during the first quarter of 1944) gave rise to the idea of establishing a flying unit consisting of Russian voluntary personnel in the Luftwaffe.

Within the scope of *Ergänzungs-Nachtschlachtgruppe Ostland Luftflotte 1* also organized a *Staffel* manned by Russian volunteers, ie *Ostfliegerstaffel (russisch)* in December 1943. The equipment consisted of ex-Soviet Polikarpov Po-2s and Yakovlev UT-2s, and also a number of Arado Ar 66s and Gotha Go 145s. In the beginning of 1944 the *Staffel* was located in Dünaburg (Daugavpils) in Latvia, and subordinated to *3 Fliegerdivision*. In March 1944 the *Staffel* was transferred to *Luftflotte 6* (subordinated to *Fliegerführer 1*) and relocated to Lida in Belorussia, and was finally disbanded in July 1944, after performing a total of over 500 missions. This *Staffel* operated successfully against Soviet partisans in Belorussia with nine war-booty Polikarpov Po-2s (U-2s).

In 1944-45 the active Gerhard Buschmann was also to participate in organizing the VVS ROA; ie the Air Force of the *Russkaya Osvoboditel'naya Armiya* or the "Russian Liberation Army", created by Col-Gen. Andrej A. Vlasov.[23] Half-heartedly supported by the Germans (who were primarily interested in only his propaganda value, Vlasov attempted to organise an anti-Stalin Russian liberation army among Soviet prisoners of war in Germany. *Oberleutnant* Buschmann became the adjutant of General Heinrich Aschenbrenner (German Air Attache in Moscow before the war), who was *"Inspizient für Ausländisches Personal der Luftwaffe Ost"* (his title has been presented simpler as *"General der Ostflieger"* in some sources).

The CO of the VVS ROA was Maj-Gen. Viktor I. Maltsev, former CO of the Air Force of the Siberian Military District, with Col. A.F. Vanyushkin, former CO of the Air Force of the Soviet 20th Army, as his Chief of Staff. (The 20th Army — commanded by Vlasov! — had fought gallantly against the Germans during the battle of Moscow late autumn 1941).

The formation of the 1. Regiment of VVS ROA (CO Col. L.I. Bajdak) started in February 1945 at Eger (now Cheb) in Bohemia, and the first two squadrons were ready for action in mid-April 1945:

(Please note that different numbers are used for the Russian and German unit designations.)

1. istrebitel 'naya eskadrilya imeni polkovnika Kazakova (*Jagdstaffel 5 "Oberst Kazakov"* commanded by Maj. HSU Semyon T. Bychkov (formerly deputy CO 482 1AP, HSU 2.9.1943) and equipped with 16 Me 109G-10 fighters.

This squadron was named after the No 1 fighter ace of the Imperial Russian Air Force Aleksandr A. Kazakov with 17 confirmed victories in the First World War. After the Bolshevik Revolution on 7 November 1917 he joined the White forces and commanded the joint Russo-British Squadron in North Russia. On 3 August 1919 Kazakov deliberately crashed to his death after the British decision to withdraw from Russia was announced.

2. eskadrilya bombardirovschchikov (*Schlachtstaffel 8*) commanded by Capt. HSU Bronislav R. Antilevskiy. Because of the total air supremacy of the Soviet AF,

---

[23] Former CO of the Soviet 2nd Shock Army, taken prisoner on 12 July 1942, after his Army had been surrounded and destroyed at the Volkhov Front.

day missions had hardly any prospects of success, and consequently the squadron was converted into an *eskadrilya nochnykh bombardirovshchikov (Nachtschlachtstaffel)* on 28 March 1945. It was equipped with 12 Ju 88 bombers.

(It is somewhat surprising to note that both in the contemporary wartime propaganda and in the post-war emigré literature describing the Vlasov movement Bychkov and Antilevskiy are proudly presented as *Heroes of the Soviet Union* regardless of the self-evident anti-communist nature of these publications — indicating both that this decoration was not considered primarily a political one, but symbolized utmost personal courage, respected by both sides. It is also a fact that soldiers who had earned this highest Soviet decoration and had joined the Vlasov movement were used as examples for recruiting purposes by the VVS ROA propagandists! Bychkov and Antilevskiy were however obviously immediately stripped of their Soviet decorations when it became known that they had joined the Vlasov movement, and their names are missing from the two-volume Soviet encyclopedia presenting all Heroes of the Sovet Union, published in 1987-88).

Aircraft had also been allocated to the following units of VVS ROA:

3. Razvedyvatel 'naya eskadrilya (Aufklärungsstaffel — Capt. S. Artemov) — three Fieseler Fi 156s and one Messerschmitt Me 262 (!) for photo reconnaissance,

4. Transportnaya eskadrilya (Transportstaffel — Maj. M. Tarnovskiy), with two Junkers Ju 52s, and finally the

5. Uchebno-trenirovachnaya eskadrilya (Ausbildungsstaffel — also commanded by Maj. M. Tarnovskiy) with two Me 109s, two Ju 88s, two Fi 156s, two Polikarpov Po-2s, one He 111 and one Do 17.

Only one combat mission of the VVS ROA is however known — the *2. Eskadrilya nochnykh bombardirovshchikov* supported the attack of the 1. Division of ROA (commanded by Maj-Gen. S.K. Bunyachenko) against the Soviet bridgehead at Erlenhof south of Fürstenhof on 13 April 1945.

The lack of serviceable aircraft and especially fuel during the last weeks of the Second World War in Germany seriously reduced the operational possibilities of the VVS ROA in April 1945 — not to mention the lack of trust these Russians continually faced from the German authorities.

The national identification symbol of the VVS ROA consisted of the blue St. Andrew's cross on white background applied on fuselage and wings. No photographs of ROA aircraft seem to exist however.

The end of the short history of the VVS ROA was very tragic. At the Yalta conference in February 1945 the Americans and British had naively promised to exchange all "displaced persons" with the Soviets. Although many ROA units and personnel tried to surrender to Western forces the front-line commanders were not prepared to meet Russian soldiers in German uniforms — they could not even distinguish between "allied Red Army units" and the fiercely anti-Soviet ROA-troops, with both groups speaking Russian . . . In most cases the ROA troops were subsequently handed over to the Soviet NKVD who treated them with their well-known efficiency . . .

During the last days of April 1945 Capt. Antilevskiy had a long-distance aircraft at stand-by ready to transport Vlasov to a neutral country, Spain or Portugal, in order to continue the negotiations with the Western powers on a higher diplomatic level. Vlasov however declined to accept this opportunity to escape at the last moment, and was subsequently captured by Soviet troops on 12 May 1945 near Schlüsselburg fortress in Bohemia when returning from a fruitless meeting with American forces. Maltsev had succeeded in surrendering to the Americans and was interrogated in Germany and France, but as soon as the Soviets became aware of his existence, they demanded that the Americans hand him over. Despite two unsuccessful suicide attempts he was finally transported from Paris to Moscow in May 1946.

Twelve leaders of the ROA (including Vlasov and Maltsev) were executed in Moscow on 1 August 1946, as German defectors in the Red Air Force.

On 26 April 1945 *Luftflotte 6* reported shooting down an Fw 190 with a red *Balkenkreuz* (!) under the wings, "Soviet star" on the fuselage and a black-white-red cockade on the tail. This insignia was verified through downing. Pilot — probably German — dead.

In Germany there has recently been some discussion whether this could have been a pilot of the so-called 'Seydlitz unit' from the anti-Fascist *Nationalkomittee Freies Deutschland* formed in the Soviet Union. *General der Artillerie* Walther von Seydlitz-Kurzbach (CO of the LI. Army Corps of the 6th Army of von Paulus) was imprisoned after the capitulation of *Generalfeldmarschall* Friedrich von Paulus at Stalingrad on 31 January 1943. Seydlitz later became the Chairman of the anti-Fascist *Bund deutscher Offizieren* set up among imprisoned German officers in the Soviet Union.

A number of leaflet dropping operations by alleged 'Seydlitz pilots' over Breslau in February-March 1945, and encounters in the Berlin area in April 1945 are also reported by various Luftwaffe personnel. The aircraft used by the enemy were reportedly Messerschmitt Bf 109s and Focke-Wulf Fw 190s using a unique combination of the *Balkenkreuz* and hammer-and-sickle insignia.

Other aircraft mentioned to have been flown by "Seydlitz-pilots" in the Riga area in February 1945 are Gotha Go 145 and Focke-Wulf Fw 44 Stieglitz.

APPENDIX 4

Luftwaffe aircraft transferred to the USSR by Finland

Of the many German-made aircraft used by the Finnish Air Force in the so-called "Continuation War", four ended their days on the Soviet side in a more or less serviceable condition.

One Heinkel He-115 used for transport of long-range patrols beyond the front line was lost at a forced landing 100 km east of Lake Onega on 4 July 1943. Three months later this aircraft was seen dismantled by a Finnish long-range patrol at the Sekee railway station, and might thus, at least theoretically, still have flown in Soviet colours.

Three other aircraft, another Heinkel He-115, an Arado Ar 196 and a Focke-Wulf Fw 58 – all German-registered but on loan from the *Luftwaffe* to the Finnish Air Force for long-range patrol tasks, and thus flown and maintained by Finnish crews – had, according to the Soviet-Finnish armistice treaty signed on 19 September 1944, to be handed over to the Soviet Union as German property. As these aircraft were still much needed by the Finnish Air Force against the former allies during the Lapland war, they were given temporary Finnish civil registrations. This did not escape the Soviet Control Commission, which required the transfer of these aircraft as according to the treaty they were German property. Forty-eight railway cars loaded with "aircraft material", 92 cars with aircraft bombs, 14 cars with a dismounted hangar from Viitana etc. (out of a total of 163 cars with ex-German war-booty armament) were handed over to the Soviet authorities at Lappeenranta in south-eastern Finland on 25 November 1944. Finland had also to deliver all maps and related material (air photographs, etc.) concerning areas east of the new Finnish-Soviet border. The map deliveries consisted of 16 million maps, requiring a total of 38 railway cars!

The ex-Norwegian Heinkel He-115A-2 (coded HE-115 in the Finnish Air Force) was used to transport Finnish long-range patrols beyond the frontline into the Soviet East Carelia. This aircraft was WNr. 3038, No 156 (F.50) of the Norwegian Naval Air Force, and had arrived in Petsamo, the northern-most part of Finland, to where the Norwegian Ltn. Helge Dahl had escaped from Tromsö on 8 June 1940 after the capitulation of the Norwegian forces in the far north. The aircraft was interned in Finland and subsequently taken over by the Finnish Air Force. HE-115, which was called *Jenny* in Finland, was lost on 4 July 1943 when Ltn Yrjö Lemminki of LeLv 44 was to bring home a long-range patrol which had been "out" since 16 June. Ltn Lemminki did not find the intended meeting point but made a forced-landing at the reserve spot, Lake Tugasjärvi, approximately 100 km east of Lake Onega, after being fired on by Soviet troops. The three-man crew of the He-115 were taken prisoners, and the long-range patrol had to wait until 10 July, when they were brought home by another aircraft, except for two of the patrol members who tried to reach the Finnish lines by foot. When finally reaching the front line on 18 July 1943, they unfortunately stood on a mine which killed one of the two men, while the other was rescued by Finnish soldiers. On 6 July 1943 two Finnish Morane-Saulnier MS.406 fighters tried to destroy the unfortunate HE-115 without success, and it was finally seen dismounted at Sekee railway station by another Finnish long-range patrol on 3 October 1943. The crew of HE-115 returned to Finland from the Soviet PoW camp on 22 November 1944.

In Spring 1943, the Finnish Air Force got two more He-115s on loan from the *Luftwaffe*: 6H+BK and 6H+CK. The latter was one evacuated by the Germans in September 1944 after the Finnish-Soviet armistice, but 6H+BK was used by the Finnish Air Force during the so-called Lapland war against the retreating German troops in northern Finland, this time transporting Finnish long-distance patrols into the **German** rear! At the end of September 1944 it was given both Finnish military (HE-116) and unofficial, out-of-sequence civil registration, OH-PMJ. The German origin of this aircraft did, however, not escape the watchful eyes of the Allied (i.e. Soviet) Control Commissions supervising the fulfilment of the armistice conditions, and on 22 November 1944 it was flown to Santahamina, Helsinki, where it was dismantled. It was subsequently delivered to the Soviet Union on 16 March 1945 (as were one Ar 196 and a Fw 58). Its total flight time was 704 hours.

Another He-115, 8L+IH of 1./Ku.Fl.Gr. 906, was lost on 22 October 1942, when it flew out from Pälläjärvi, Hirvas in East Carelia to bring home a long-distance patrol consisting of Estonian volunteers in the Finnish Army. This aircraft was flown by a pure German crew, and can thus not be considered as belonging to the Finnish Air Force as the 6H+BK mentioned above. This patrol had jumped by parachute, landing at Lake Latshajärvi, near Konosha (at the Arkhangelsk-Vologda railway, east of Lake Onega) from a German Junkers Ju 52 (BA+KG of TGr 20) which had taken off from Nurmoila on 30 August 1942 (this was the first operational parachute jump in the history of the Finnish Army). The task of the patrol was to record the traffic on the Arkhangelsk-Vologda railway, which carried Anglo-American lend-lease arms deliveries from the important White Sea port to the Red Army. (According to Soviet sources, the task of the "saboteurs" was to "isolate the Soviet northern regions from the central regions by cutting the supply lines, and advance from Konosha to Vologda in the south.")

Some years ago it was revealed that the unfortunate patrol had been detected by Soviet NKVD troops at an early stage, and a number of soldiers were killed in the fighting while others had been captured. The radio-operators had been "turned around", and the He-115 crew were thus immediately caught by the NKVD at Lake Jungozero. The aircraft was only slightly damaged in the left engine, and was inspected by "aviation specialists" together with the NKVD troops. Two crew members and the leader of the *Abwehr* operation, who flew out as passenger, had been killed. The third crew member committed suicide when being caught. No-one of this thirteen-man patrol returned – the unfortunate patrol included virtually the entire Estonian national rifle shooting team which had won the gold medals at the World Championship at Luzern, Switzerland, in 1939. Nothing further is known about the fate of this aircraft, except that it was inspected by "aviation specialists" together with the NKVD troops immediately after capture – which might indicate that the aircraft included some interesting special equipment.

Arado Ar 196
A total of three Arado Ar 196A-3s were given on loan to the Finnish Air Force by the *Luftwaffe* (flown by Finnish crews, but in the original German colours); one Ar 196 (GA + DO) was used during the summer of 1943, and two in 1944. Of these, one (A3 + BC) was returned to the Germans in September 1944, while the other (A3 + AC) was used by the Finnish Air Force during the Lapland War against the retreating German forces in northern Finland, being used for the transportation of long-range patrols, evacuating of wounded, etc. It was given the unofficial, out-of-sequence Finnish civil registration OH-PMK. The German origin of this aircraft did, however, not escape the watchful eyes of the Allied (i.e. Soviet) Control Commission supervising the fulfilment of the armistice conditions, and it was thus on 22 November 1944 flown to Santahamina, Helsinki, where it was temporarily stored. It was dismantled on 7 March 1945, and subsequently delivered to the Soviet Union on 16 March 1945 (likewise one He-115 and one Fw 58). Its total flight time was 570 hours.

Two Gotha Go 242 transport gliders were used by a detachment of the German 3./KG 200 (*1. Seekommando,* commanded by *Hauptmann* Theodor Queens) located at Rissala, Kuopio, in eastern Finland in summer 1944. These transport gliders, which were left behind by the Germans in September 1944, were subsequently handed over to the Soviet Union in late autumn 1944. (Most of the other aircraft used by *1. Seekommando* were evacuated by the Germans, i.e. three Leore 246 flying-boats, one Heinkel He-115 and one Arado Ar 196 floatplane.)

Focke-Wulf Fw 58 Weihe

One Focke-Wulf Fw 58 Weihe (NH + OI) was given on loan to the Finnish Air Force by the *Luftwaffe* (flown by a Finnish crew, but in the original German colours) in 1943. It was used for VIP transports by the Finnish Army intelligence department (which i.e. was responsible for the long-range patrols into the Soviet rear, also using aircraft on loan from *Luftwaffe* in addition to the aircraft placed at its disposal by the Finnish Air Force). After the Finnish-Soviet armistice at the beginning of September 1944, the Fw 58 was still used for some time in the "Lapland War" against the retreating German forces in northern Finland, with both Finnish military (FH-1) and unofficial out-of-sequence civil registrations (OH-PMS).

The German origin of this aircraft did, however, not escape the watchful eyes of the Allied (i.e. Soviet) Control Commission supervising the fulfilment of the armistice conditions, and it was thus on 24 November 1944 flown to Malmi airport, Helsinki, then used by the Soviet Control Commission (at that time served as home base of the 4 Guards IAP of the Baltic Fleet, commanded by one of the most famous aces of the Naval Air Forces, HSU Lt.-Col. Vasiliy F. Golubev). According to unconfirmed rumours, it never did reach the Soviet Union proper, as the Soviet soldiers are said to have set it on fire!

SOURCES

1. General references

Agoston, T.: *Blunder: How the U.S. gave away Nazi super-secrets to the Russians,* Dodd, Mead & Co., New York, 1985.

Akten zur deutschen auswärtigen Politik, Serie D (1937-1945), Band VII-XII; *Baden-Baden,* Frankfurt-am-Main, Bonn, Göttingen 1956 . . . 1969.

Alexander, J.P. and Voaden, D.J.: *Foreign Aircraft in Russian Service, Air Pictorial,* December 1959, January 1960.

Alexander, J.: *Russian Aircraft since 1940,* Putnam, London 1975.

Andersson, L.: *Secret Luftwaffe, Air Enthusiast No. 41* (1990).

Aviatsiya i kosmonavtika SSSR, Voyenizdat, Moskva 1968.

Barbas, B.: *Planes of the Luftwaffe Fighter Aces,* 2 volumes, Kookaburra, Melbourne 1985.

Bower, T.: *The Paperclip Conspiracy,* Grafton, London 1988.

Boyle, W.J: *Messerschmitt Me 262,* Smithsonian Institution Press, Washington, D.C., 1982.

Die deutsche Luftfahrt:

Band 2: K. von Gersdorff, K. Grasmann: *Flugmotoren und Strahltriebwerke,* Bernard & Graefe, Koblenz 1981.

Band 5: H.D. Köhler: *Ernst Heinkel — Pionier der Schnellflugzeuge,* Bernard & Graefe, Koblenz 1983.

Band 14: W. Wagner: *Die ersten Strahlflugzeuge der Welt,* Bernard & Graefe, Koblenz 1989.

Band 15: R. Cescotti: *Kampfflugzeuge und Aufklärer — von 1935 bis zur Gegenwart,* Bernard & Graefe, Koblenz 1989.

Eyermann, K.H.: *Die Luftfahrt der UdSSR,* Transpress, Berlin (DDR) 1977 and 1983.

Foreman, J., Harvey, S.E.: *The Messerschmitt Me 262 combat diary,* Air Research, New Malden 1990.

Friedensburg, F.: *Die sowjetischen Kriegslieferungen an das Hitlerreich,* Vierteljahrshefte fur Wirtschaftsforschung, S. 331-338, Berlin 1962.

Geroi Sovetskogo Soyuza (2 volumes), Voyenizdat 1987-1988.

Geust, C.F. et al: *Red Stars in the Sky, Vol. 1-3,* Tietoteos, Espoo 1979-1983.

Green, W.: *Warplanes of the Third Reich,* Macdonald, London 1970.

Green, W., Swanborough, G.: *Soviet Air Force Fighters (2 Parts),* Macdonald, London 1977, 1978.

La Guerre d'Espagne, tome 1 et 2, ICARE 118 and 130, Paris 1986 and 1989.

Gunston, B.: *Aircraft of the Soviet Union,* Osprey, London 1983.

Hardesty, V.: *Red Phoenix,* Smithsonian Institution Press, Washington, D.C., 1982.

Heinkel, E.: *Stürmisches Leben, Mundus-Verlag,* Stuttgart 1953.

Howson, G.: *Aircraft of the Spanish Civil War,* Putnam, London 1990.

Ivanitskiy, G.M.: *Sovetsko-germanskoiye torgovo-ekonomicheskiye otnosheniya v 1939-1941 gg.,* Novaya i novejshaya istoriya, no. 5/1989.

K istorii zaklyucheniya sovetsko-germanskogo dogovora o nenapadenii 23 avgusta 1939 g., Novaya i novejshaya istoriya, no. 6/1989.

Keller, W.: *Ost minus West* = Null, Knaur, 1968.

Kurowski, F.: *Unternehmen Paperclip,* Langen-Müller, München 1982.

Lange, B.: *Das Buch der deutschen Luftfahrtstechnik (2 Bände),* Dieter Hoffman, Mainz 1970.

Laureau, P.: *La aviacion Respublicana Española 1936-1939 (2 volumes).*

Masters, D.: *German Jet Genesis,* Jane's, London 1982.

Miller, R.: *The Soviet Air Force,* Time-Life Books, Alexandra VA 1983.

Nemecek, V.: *Sowjetflugzeuge* Walther Zuerl, Steinebach-Wörthsee

Nemecek, V.: *Soviet aircraft from 1918,* Willow Book, London 1986.

Nowarra, H.J., Duval, G.R.: *Russian civil and military aircraft 1884-1969,* Fountain Press, London 1971.

Nowarra, H.J.: *Die deutsche Luftrüstung 1933-1945, (4 Bände),* Bernard & Graefe, Koblenz 1985-1988.

Price, A: *The Luftwaffe 1933-1945 (4 Volumes),* Arm & Armour Press 1981-1982.

Ries, K., Ring, H.: *Legion Condor,* Dieter Hoffmann, Mainz 1980.

Shavrov, V.B.: *Istoriya konstruktsiy samoletov v SSSR do 1938 goda,* Mashinostroyeniye, Moskva 1968, 1978 and 1986.

Shavrov, V.B.: *Istoriya konstruktsiy samoletov v SSSR 1938-1950 gg.,* Mashinostroyeniye, Moskva 1978 and 1988.

Shores, C.: *Luftwaffe Fighter Units Russia 1941-1945.* Aircam/Airwar 11, Osprey, London 1978.

Smith, J.R., Creek, E.J.: *Jet planes of the Third Reich,* Monogram, Boylston 1982.

Soviet-German Military Cooperation, 1920-1933, International Affairs no 7/1990.

Sutton, A.C.: *Western Technology and Soviet Economic Development 1917-30,* Hoover Institution Press, Stanford CA, 1968.

Sutton, A.C.: *Western Technology and Soviet Economic Development 1930-45,* Hoover Institution Press, Stanford CA, 1971.

Sutton, A.C.: *Western Technology and Soviet Economic Development 1945-65*, 1973.

Tokayev, G.A.: *Stalin Means War,* Weidenfeld & Nicolson, London, 1951.

Tokayev, G.A.: *Comrade X,* Harvill Press, London, 1956.

2. Specific references.

Abraimov, I.: *Polveka v nebe Kirgizii,* Kyrgyzstan, Frunze, 1982.

Agranovskiy, A.: *Raznaya smelost',* Detgiz, Moskva 1961.

Akkuratov, V.I.: *V pervuyu osen' posle vojny* Vokrug sveta No. 8/1980.

Akkuratov, V.I.: *Led i pepel,* Sovremennik, Moskva 1984.

Alexandrov, A.O., Franzke, M., Griehl, M.: *Das Geheimunis der Ju 287V 3,* Flugzeug no 2/1991.

Alexandrov, A.O., Griehl, M.: *Die Geheime entwicklung der DFS 346,* Flugzeug no 7/1991.

Alexandrov, A.O., Griehl, M.: *Die zweisitzige Me 163,* Flugzeug no 6/1991.

O.K. Antonov. Planery. Samolety., Naukova dumka, Kiyev 1990.

Anttonen, O.: *Luftwaffe Suomessa — in Finland, Vol. 2*, Helsinki 1980.

Arias, A.: *V ognennom nebe,* Belarus, Minsk 1988.

Arlazorov, M.S.: *Front idet cherez KB,* Znaniye 1975.

Arlazorov, M.S.: *Artyom Mikoyan,* Molodaya Gvardiya 1978.

Armejskiye chekisty, Lenizdat, Leningrad 1985.

Belyakov, A.V.: *V polet skvoz gody,* Voyenizdat, Moskva 1981.

Bogdanov, N.G.: *V nebe — gvardeyskiy Gatchinskiy,* Lenizdat, Leningrad 1980.

Bondarenko, B.: *V vozsdukhe — ispytateli,* DOSAAF, 1975.

Brandner, F.: *Die Entwicklung der Propellerturbine in der Sowjetunion, MTZ* Jahrg. 18 (1957), No. 8, S. 261.

Brandner, F.: *Die Propellerturbine-entwicklung in der Sowjetunion, Schw. Bauzeitung* 75 (1957), Nr. 32, 33, S. 508-511, 520-524.

Brandner, F.: *Ein Leben zwischen den Fronten,* Verlag Wesermühl 1973.

Brazhnin, I.Ya.: *V velikoj otechestvennoj,* Voyenizdat, Moskva 1971.

Burov, A.V.: *Ognennoye nebo,* Lenizdat, Leningrad 1974.

Chechel 'nitskiy, G.A.: *Letchiki na vojne,* Voyenizdat, Moskva 1974.

Chuyev, F.: *Stechkin, Molodaya gvardiya,* Moskva 1978.

Dvoryanskiy, Ye.M., Yaroshenko, A.A.: *V ognennom koltse, Eesti raamat,* Tallinn 1977.

Eesti riik ja rahvas teises maailmasojas, VII, EMP, Stockholm 1959.

Ekononov, L.: *Kapitan Vandzhi,* DOSAAF, Moskva 1972.

Fedorov, A.G.: *Do poslednogo starta,* Voyenizdat, Moskva 1965.

Fedorov, A.G.: *V nebe — pikirovshchiki,* DOSAAF, Moskva 1986.

Gaj, D.: *Vertolety zovutsya MI,* Moskovskiy rabochiy, Moskva 1973, 1976.

Gaj, D.: *Profil' krylya,* Moskovskiy rabochiy, Moskva 1981.

Gaj, D.: *Nebesnoye prityazheniye,* Moskovskiy rabochiy, Moskva 1984.

Gallaj, M.L.: *Cherez nevidimyye baryery* — Ispitany v nebe, Molodaya gvardiya 1965. (German translation: Über unsichtbare Barrieren, Militärverlag, Berlin (DDR), 1968).

Gallaj, M.L.: *Tretye izmereniye,* Sovetskiy pisatel', Moskva 1979.

Gellermann, G.: *Moskau ruft Heeresgruppe Mitte . . .,* Bernard & Graefe, Koblenz 1988

Golubev, G.G.: *V pare s "sotym",* DOSAAF 1974 and 1978.

Grazhdanskaya aviatsiya SSSR 1917-1967, Transport, Moskva 1967.

Grazdanskiy vozdushnyy flot v Velikoj Otechestvennoj vojne, Vozdushnyy transport, Moskva 1985.

Hitchcock, T.H.: *Junkers Ju 287,* Monogram Close-Up 1, Acton MA, 1974.

Hoffmann, J.: *Die Geschichte der Wlassov-Armee,* Rombach, Freiburg, 1984.

Ikh pozvalo nebo, Voyenizdat, Moskva 1984 (History of the Borisoglebsk Military Flying School).

Ilyuin, N.G., Rulin, V.D.: *Gvardejtsy v vozdukhe,* DOSAAF, Moskva 1973.

Istoriya grazhdanskoy aviatsii SSSR, Vozdushnyy transport, Moskva 1983.

Ivanov, A.L.: *Skorost', manevr, orgon',* DOSAAF, Moskva 1974.

Jack, V.W.: *Die Junkers Ju 287 and ihre weiteren Entwicklung EF 131,* Aviatik No 2 and 3, 1990-91

Kaberov, I.A.: *V pritsele svastika,* Lenizdat, Leningrad 1975 and 1983.

Kalinin, A.P.: *Istrebiteli nad "goluboj linyej",* Voyenizdat, Moskva 1963.

Kazakov, V.B.: *Sotvori sebya,* Saratov 1980.

Kazakov, V.B.: *A-7 ukhodyat v noch',* DOSAAF 1981.

Kazakov, V.B.: *Boyevyje aerostsepki,* DOSAAF 1988.

(Kerber, L.L.): *Tupolevskaya sharaga,* Posev, Frankfurt/Main 1971 (published under the pseudonym A. Sharagin — then erroneously assumed to be G.A. Ozerov).

Kerber, L.L.: *Tu — chelovek i samolet,* Sovetskaya Rossiya, Moskva 1973.

Kerber, L.L.: *A delo shlo k vojne . . .* Izobretatel' i ratsionalizator, no. 3-9, 1988; 5-9/1990.

Kerber, L.L.: *Tupolevskaya sharaga,* Teknikha i nauka, no 1-/1990.
(from no 6/1990 the name of the journal was changed to "Inzhener").

Keskinen, K. et al: *Fokker D.XXI (History of the Finnish Air Force, Vol. 3),* Tietoteos, Helsinki 1974 and Espoo 1977.

Kindyushev, I.I.: *K pobednym rassvetam,* Voyenidat, Moskva 1978.

Koyander, Ye.V.: *Ya — "Rubin", prikazyvayu . . .,* Voyenizdat 1978.

Kozhedub, I.: *Sluzhu rodine,* Leningrad 1950.

Kozhedub, I.: *Vernost' otchizne, Detskaya literatura,* Moskva 1970; Voyenizdat, Moskva 1975.

Kozhevnikov, A.L.: *Startuyet muzhestvo,* Voyenizdat, Moskva 1966 and 1975.

Kozhevnikova T., Popovich M.: *Pesn' vysoty,* DOSAAF, Moskva 1980.

Krasovskiy, S.A.: *Zhizn' v aviatsii,* Voyenizdat 1968.

Krylya rodiny, Politizdat, Moskva 1979 and 1982.

Krylya rodiny, DOSAAF, Moskva 1983.

Kuznetsov, V.A.: *Serebryannyye krylya,* Voyenizdat, Moskva 1972.

Kuz'mina, L.M.: *Ognennoye serdtse,* Moskovskiy rabochiy, Moskva 1983.

Kuz'mina, L.M.: *General 'nyj konstruktor Pavel Sukhoj,* Molodaya Gvardiya, Moskva 1983; Belarus',
    Kiyev 1985.

Lavrinenkov, V.D.: *Vozvrazheniye v nebo,* Voyenizdat, Moskva 1974 and 1983.

Lavrinenkov, V.D.: *Sokol-1,* DOSAAF, Moskva 1976.

Lavrinenkov, V.D.: *Bez vojny,* Politizdat Ukrainy, Kiyev 1982.

Lavrinenkov, V.D., Belovol, N.N.: *Shpaga chesti,* Politizdat Ukrainy, Kiyev 1982.

Lazarev, L.L.: *Vzlet, Profizdat,* Moskva 1978.

Lazarev, L.L.: *Kosnuvshis' neba,* Profizdat, Moskva 1983.

Letchiki, Molodaya Gvardiya, Moskva 1978.

Luganskiy, S.D.: *Na glubokikh virazhakh,* Zhazushy, Alma-Ata 1966.

Luganskiy, S.D.: *Nebo ostayetsya chistym,* Zhazushy, Alma-Ata1970.

Lyudi bessmertnogo podviga, tom 1, Politizdat, Moskva 1975.

Lyudi geroicheskoj professii, DOSAAF, Moskva 1977.

Mäkelä, J.: *Salaisen sodan saatosta,* WSOY, Porvoo 1965

Merono, F.: *I snova v boj,* Voyenizdat, Moskva 1977.

Mikhajlik, Ya.D.: *Sokolnaya sem'ya,* Voyenizdat, Moskva 1971.

Mikhajlov, P.M.: *Nebo pokoryayetsya sil'nym,* Molodaya Gvardiya, Moskva 1984.

Mikhalenko, K.F.: *Sluzhu nebo,* Belarus', Minsk 1980.

Moiseyev, V.A.: *Krylatoye imya,* Dnipro, Kiyev 1974.

Muravyev, V.K.: *Ispytaleli VVS,* Voenizdat, Moskva 1990.

Na krayu neba, Khabarovsk 1976.

Nekotoryye daty k istorii TsAGI, Mashinostroyeniye, Moskva 1978.

Nemirova, M., Avaliani, Yu.: **Skvoz' gody na krylyakh,** Savchota sakartvelo, Tbilisi 1973.

Nykänen-H. Rytky: *Kuopion lentoaseman historia I,* Kuopio 1985

Oruzhiye pobedy, Mashinostroyeniye, Moskva 1987.

Ovcharenko, Ye.V.: *Na frontovykh aerodromakh,* Voyenizdat, Moskva 1975.

Petrov, I.: *Schitayu dolgom rasskazat', Izobretatel' i ratsionalizator,* no 11/1984; 3,4/1986.

Pflugel, K: *Schicksale deutscher Luftfahrtingenieure,* Selbstverlag, Diesen 1975.

Plyushchov, B.: *General Maltsev,* SBONR, San Fransisco, 1982.

Pokryshkin, A.I.: *Nebo vojny,* Voyenizdat, Moskva 1966, 1980.

(German translation: *Pokryschkin, A.: Himmel des Krieges,* Militärverlag, Berlin (DDR), 1978.

Pokryshkin, A.I.: *Poznat' sebya v boyu,* DOSAAF 1986.

Polarnyy krug, Mysl, Moskva 1984.

Polynin, F.P.: *Boyevyye marshruty,* Voyenizdat, Moskva 1972 and 1981.

Ponomaryev, A.N.: *Sovetskiye aviatsionnyye konstruktory,* Voyenizdat, Moskva 1977, 1980 and 1990.

Popovich, M.: *Khozhdeniye za dva makha,* Sovetskaya Rossiya, Moskva 1981.

Presyakov, A.V.: *Nad volnami Baltiki,* Voyenizdat, Moskva 1979; Lenizdat, Leningrad 1983.

Pstygo, I.I.: *Na boyevom kurse,* Voyenizdat, Moskva 1989.

Puzyrev, V.P.: *Belomorskaya flotiliya v Velikoj Otechestvennoj vojne,* Voyenizdat 1981.

Rabkin, I.G.: *Vremya, lyudi,* **samolety,** Moskovskiy rabochiy, Moskva 1985.

Radtke, S.: *Kampfgeschwader 54,* Schild Verlag, München 1990

Radzicki, F.: **Der Vergessene Jet,** Flugzeug no 1/1992

Rislakki, J.: *Erittäin salainen,* Love kirjat, Helsinki 1982

Ritaranta, E. – Mäkinen, T.: *The Complete Civil Aircraft Registers of Finland,* Air-Britain Archive Special No 5, 1992

Romanov, R.B.: *Vzlet, Detskaya literatura,* Leningrad 1985.

Rudenko, S.I.: *Krylya pobedy,* Voyenizdat, Moskva 1976 and 1985.

Saburov, S.P.: *Vsegda soldat,* Voyenizdat, Moskva 1963.

Saressalo, L.: *Päämajan kaukopartiot jatkosodassa,* WSOY, Juva 1987

Savchenko, V.I.: *Latyshskiye formirovaniya Sovetskoj Armii na frontakh Velikoj Otechestvennoj vojny,* Zinatne, Riga 1975.

Savitskiy, Ye. Ya.: *V nebe nad Maloj zemlej,* Ogonek, Moskva 1979; Krasnodarsk 1980.

Savitskiy, Ye. Ya.: *Nebo dlya smelykh,* DOSAAF, Moskva 1985.

Savitskiy, Ye. Ya.: *Ya — "Drakon — Atakuyu!",* Molodaya gvardiya, Moskva 1988.

Savitskiy, Ye. Ya.: *Polveka s nebom,* Voyenizdat, Moskva 1988.

Semyonov, A.F.: *Na vzlete,* Voyenidat, Moskva 1969.

Semyonov, A.F., Dashtseren, B.: *Eskadriliya "Mongolskiy Arat",* Voyenidat, Moskva 1978.

17-ya vozdushnaya armiya v boyakh ot Stalingrada do Veny, Voyenizdat, Moskva 1977.

Shakhurin, A.I.: *Krylya pobedy,* Politizdat, Moskva 1983 and 1990 (German translation: A.I. Schachurin: Flügel des Sieges, Militärverlag, Berlin (DDR), 1989).

Shelest', I.I.: *Lechu za mechtoj,* Molodaya gvardiya, Moskva 1973.

Shelest', I.I.: *S kryla na krylo,* Molodaya gvardiya, Moskva 1977.

Shelest', I.I.: *Krylatyye lyudi,* Moskovskiy rabochiy, 1980.

Shepelev, A.L.: *V nebe i na zemle,* Vovenizdat, Moskva 1974.

16-aya vozdushnaya, Voyenizdat, Moskva 1973.

Shevchuk, V.M.: *Komandir atakuyet pervym,* Voyenizdat, Moskva 1980.

Shinkarenko, F.I.: *Ispytany ognem,* Avots, Riga 1984.

Shkola shturmuyushchikh nebo, Krasnodar 1978.

Silantyev, V.: *Vozdushnyye razvedchiki,* Molodaya gvardiya 1983.

Sivkov, G.: *Gotovnost' nomer odin,* Sovetskaya Rossiya, Moskva 1973.

Sokoly, Lenizdat, Leningrad 1971.

Sorokin, Z.: *Zvezdy na fyuzelyazhe,* DOSAAF, Moskva 1977.

SSSR v Velikoj Otechestvennoj vojne 1941-1945, Voyenizdat, Moskva 1970.

Stefanovskiy, P.S.: *Trista neizvestnykh,* Voyenizdat, Moskva 1968 and 1973.

Strugatskiy, V.: *Vperedi — ledovaya razvedka,* Gidrometeoizdat, Leningrad 1984.

Tatarenko, V., Bondarenko, V.: *Za oblakami — solntse!,* Rostov 1973.

Tishchenko, A.T.: *Vedomyyje "Drakona",* Voyenizdat, Moskva 1966.

Tsykin, A.D.: *Ot "Ilyi Muromtsa do raketonostsa",* Voyenizdat 1975.

Vishnyakov, I.A.: *Na krutikh virazhakh,* Voyenizdat, Moskva 1973.

V nebe Kitaya 1937-1940, Nauka, Moskva 1980 and 1986.

V nebe — letchiki Baltiki, Eesti raamat, Tallinn 1974.

Vodopyanov, M., Grigoryevich, G.: *Letat' rozdennnyj,* DOSAAF, Moskva 1969. (Documentary biography of Yakov Smushkevich).

Vodopyanov, M.V.: *Druzya v nebe,* Sovetskaya Rossiya, 1971.

Vojska PVO strany v Velikoj Otechestvennoj vojne 1941-1945: Voyenizdat, Moskva 1981.

Vorozhejkin, A.V.: *Ryadovoj aviatsii*, DOSAAF, Moskva 1972.

Vorozhejkin, A.V.: *Poslednyye ataki*, DOSAAF, Moskva 1979.

Vorozhejkin, A.V.: *Soldaty neba*, Voyenizdat, Moskva 1986.

Wegmann, R., Widfeldt, B.: *Nödlandning Sverige!*, Nässjö, Sweden, 1991.

Widfeldt, B.: *The Luftwaffe in Sweden*, Monogram, 1983.

Yakimenko, A.D.: *V atake — "Mech"*, DOSAAF, Moskva 1973.

Yakovlev, A.S.: *O velikom o prostom cheloveke*, Detgiz, Moskva 1945.

Yakovlev, A.S.: *The Aim of a Lifetime*, Progress, Moscow, 1972.

Yakovlev, A.S.: *Rasskazy aviakonstruktora*, Detskaya literatura, Moskva 1958, 1974.

Yakovlev, A.S.: *Zapiski konstruktora*, Politizdat, Moskva 1979.

Yakovlev, A.S.: *Ziel des Lebens*, Militärverlag, Berlin (DDR), 1982.

Zakharov, G.N.: *Povest' ob istrebitelyakh*, DOSAAF, Moskva 1977.

Zakharov, G.N.: *Ya — istrebitel'*, Voyenizdat, Moskva 1985.

Zil'manovich, D.Ya., El'vikh, P.Ye.: *Latyshkij aviatsionnyj polk*, Liesma, Riga 1975.

Zil'manovich D.Ya.: *Na krylakh rodiny*, Alma-Ata 1984.

INDEX

Figures in italic type indicate photographs